PREDICTING THE MARKETS
TOPICAL STUDY #6

In Praise
of
Profits!

Edward Yardeni

YRI PRESS

Predicting the Markets Topical Study #6:
In Praise of Profits!

978-1-948025-12-6 (print)
978-1-948025-13-3 (eBook)
Library of Congress Control Number: 2021917941

Published by YRI Books, a division of Yardeni Research, Inc.
68 Wheatley Road, Suite 1100
Brookville, NY USA 11545

Contact us: **requests@yardeni.com**

Excerpted, updated, and expanded from *Predicting the Markets: A Professional Autobiography* (2018).

To my children:
Laura, David, Samuel, Sarah, and Melissa

Serve your customers well.
Profits will follow.

Author's Note

This study is another in a series of Topical Studies examining issues that I discussed in my book *Predicting the Markets: A Professional Autobiography* (2018), but in greater detail and on a more current basis. Previous studies in this series, which are available on my Amazon Author Page, include:

The Fed and the Great Virus Crisis (2021)

S&P 500 Earnings, Valuation, and the Pandemic (2020)

Fed Watching for Fun and Profit (2020)

Stock Buybacks: The True Story (2019)

The Yield Curve: What Is It Really Predicting? (2019)

The charts at the end of this study were current as of August 2021. They are available in color along with linked endnotes at **www.yardenibook.com/studies**.

Institutional investors are invited to sign up for the Yardeni Research service on a complimentary trial basis at **yardeni.com/trial**.

Contents

7 Income and Wealth in America

8 Profitable and Unprofitable Policies

Epilogue

Appendix

About the Author

Dr. Ed Yardeni is the President of Yardeni Research, Inc., a provider of global investment strategy and asset allocation analyses and recommendations. He previously served as Chief Investment Strategist of Oak Associates, Prudential Equity Group, and Deutsche Bank's US equities division in New York City. He was also the Chief Economist of CJ Lawrence, Prudential-Bache Securities, and EF Hutton. He taught at Columbia University's Graduate School of Business and was an economist with the Federal Reserve Bank of New York. He also held positions at the Federal Reserve Board of Governors and the US Treasury Department in Washington, D.C.

Dr. Ed earned his PhD in economics from Yale University in 1976, having completed his doctoral dissertation under Nobel Laureate James Tobin. Previously, he received a master's degree in international relations from Yale. He completed his undergraduate studies, *magna cum laude*, at Cornell University.

Dr. Ed is frequently quoted in the financial press, including *The Wall Street Journal*, the *Financial Times*, *The New York Times*, and *Barron's*. He was dubbed "Wall Street Seer" in a *Barron's* cover story. He appears frequently on CNBC, Fox Business, and Bloomberg Television.

"Nothing contributes so much
to the prosperity and happiness
of a country as high profits."

—*David Ricardo*

"It is a socialist idea that making
profits is a vice. I consider the
real vice is making losses."

—*Winston Churchill*

Introduction

Time to Clear Up the Confusion

There has been much confusion about corporate profits. That's because there are several measures of profits and very little understanding of, or even interest in, how they differ. As a result, there has been lots of sloppy analysis and misinformed discussion of such important issues as the central role of profits in economic growth, the trend of profits, the corporate tax rate, the profit margin, profits' share of national income, and corporate share buybacks.

The confusion has played into the hands of progressives. They claim that free-market capitalism, driven by the profit motive, causes wage stagnation and results in both income and wealth inequality. They want the government to redistribute income and wealth by increasing taxes on the rich and on corporations. They refuse to acknowledge that profit-driven capitalism is the source of our nation's widespread prosperity. They say that the relevant data support their claims; that's not so, as I demonstrate in this book. I conclude that the entrepreneurial variety of capitalism should be allowed to flourish. If it does so, so will we all.

More recently, some of these progressive critics have suggested ways to save capitalism from itself by forcing company managements to stop focusing on maximizing profits for the benefit of their shareholders. Instead, the would-be saviors of capitalism promote the idea that companies should focus on satisfying the diverse needs of their "stakeholders." This broad group includes customers, employees, vendors, communities, minorities, environmentalists, the press, and the public at large.

Progressive politicians and their economic advisers often claim that the data show that profits have gained share of national income at the expense of workers, thus causing income stagnation and exacerbating income and wealth inequality. Furthermore, they claim that corporate share buybacks represent an egregious misallocation of capital by greedy corporate executives aiming to boost their companies' earnings per share and share prices for the benefit of shareholders and to enrich themselves by driving up the value of their stock grants and options. The money would be better spent paying workers more and investing more in their companies for the benefit of their diverse stakeholders, say the progressive politicians. Yet, though they hold strong opinions on how companies ought to be managed and regulated, most have never actually run a business.

As I will show in this study, the progressives' narrative about the relationship between profits and prosperity is wrong and misleadingly pessimistic. In short, it's backward: Market-driven profit is the *source* of prosperity, not its nemesis. Ironically, profit is what drives the progress in standards of living that progressives, with their policy approaches, claim to champion. But progressives seem blind to the progress that has been achieved and perpetually want to do more. In my opinion, progress has been made despite their persistent policy interventions thanks to the power of the profit motive to deliver profits and widespread prosperity in a free-market economic system.

Meanwhile, on Wall Street prior to the pandemic, there was a different sort of misinformed view of profits: The stock market's permabears growled that corporate profits had been flat since 2012 and that profit margins had been trending down since then. They claimed that the bull market was a bubble inflated by the ultra-easy monetary policies of the Federal Reserve. After the shock of the pandemic's onset, once the bull market resumed rising to record highs, they remained convinced that it was a bubble that will eventually burst. They may very well be right, eventually, but they've been wrong so far, partly because they've misinterpreted the profits data that they have been using to make their case.

The goal of this study is to add significant clarity to the discussion of all these controversial issues by enabling more precise understanding of the crucial role that profits play in our economy. The analysis will be supported by a careful review of the underlying profits data that all too often are used misleadingly, both unintentionally and intentionally, by capitalism's critics.

Golden Goose

To be fair and balanced, I acknowledge from the get-go that income inequality is an inherent consequence of capitalism. Perversely, capitalism causes the most income inequality during periods of prosperity. The rich do get richer, but almost everyone's standard of living improves during good times. However, the wealthy get richer faster than everyone else. Entrepreneurs get richer during periods of prosperity by improving the standard of living of their customers. They do so by improving the quality, and lowering the prices, of the goods and services they offer and by creating new and better products and services. The more customers they attract, the more prosperous they become while simultaneously enriching the lives of their customers.

Here is a short list of some of the major contributions to the prosperity of Americans made by some of the most successful American entrepreneurs: railroads (Cornelius Vanderbilt), electricity (J.P. Morgan and George Westinghouse), steel (Andrew Carnegie and J.P. Morgan), kerosene and gasoline (John D. Rockefeller), automobiles (Walter Chrysler, Pierre Du Pont, Henry Ford, and J.P. Morgan Jr.), consumer credit (J.P. Morgan Jr. and Alfred Sloan), investment banking (Marcus Goldman and Samuel Sachs), commercial aviation (William Boeing and Edsel Ford), packaged foods (C.F. Birdseye II, H.J. Heinz, Milton Hershey, W.K. Kellogg, and James Kraft), fast foods (Ray Kroc and Colonel Harland Sanders), media and entertainment (William Randolph Hearst, Walt Disney, and Ted Turner), lodging (Howard Johnson and John Marriott), semiconductors (Andrew Grove), computers (Thomas Watson, Steve Jobs, and Michael Dell), software (Bill Gates), Internet search and maps (Larry Page and Sergey Brin), mutual funds (Edward C. Johnson and John C. Bogle), shipping and logistics (Fred Smith and Jeff Bezos), retailing (Richard Warren Sears, Sam Walton, and Jeff Bezos), and cloud computing (Jeff Bezos). They all got very rich by selling lots of products and services that improved their customers' lives. Most of these capitalists have set up large charitable trusts that continue to benefit lots of people in the United States and around the world.

These titans of business faced fierce competition from contemporaneous entrepreneurs. Competition forced them all to improve the quality of their offerings even as they lowered their prices. That could be done only by innovating in ways that boosted productivity. The titans were the winners of the ongoing competitive races they were in, and so were all their customers. The losers whose business gambles failed rarely get mentioned in the history books.

Keep in mind that most entrepreneurs who succeeded and became rich started out either poor or certainly much less well-off. They struck it rich by offering consumers goods and services that improved their collective well-being, often spotting consumer needs that no one else saw. So the notion that the rich and the poor constitute two distinct classes is false in a competitive, entrepreneurial capitalist economy. Enterprising individuals can become very rich indeed, but only by improving the lives of their customers. They can also fail to do so or fail once they have done so.

Capitalism is an inherently dynamic economic system. While it will always be associated with some degree of income inequality at any point in time, it also provides lots of mostly upward income mobility with plenty of opportunities both to succeed and to fail over time and to do so more than once. Persistent entrepreneurs who learn from their mistakes and failures often eventually succeed. Today's wannabe business titans can achieve their dreams. They might very well do so by coming up with a new mousetrap that puts entrenched tycoons—who got rich selling the old mousetrap—out of business.

But the reality is that most people are inclined to be workers, not entrepreneurs. Some workers can and do get poorer in competitive economies. Some lose their jobs because their companies are put out of business by competitors or unforeseen and unfortunate setbacks (such as the pandemic). Some employers are forced to move production overseas to remain in business by tapping into cheaper labor abroad. New products offered by upstarts can make older products obsolete and wipe out entire industries. In a competitive economy, workers who lose jobs can usually find opportunities for gainful employment elsewhere in the economy, especially in the industries that are flourishing. However, that might be challenging if they've been replaced with cheaper foreign labor or by automation. Their skills may no longer be in demand, forcing them to take jobs that pay less than they were making.

Over the years, progressives have made a great deal of progress in expanding the social safety net provided by the government to help people in need. Among their major achievements are Social Security, Medicare, Medicaid, Unemployment Insurance, and the Supplemental Nutrition Assistance Program. The marginal tax rates on individual incomes have been very progressive for a very long time. The tax code also includes the Earned Income Tax Credit and the Child Tax Credit. Yet ironically, progressives regularly trot out data that exaggerate both income and wealth inequality by excluding some of these programs—programs that mark their success in addressing this very issue.

Most disturbing is that progressives don't seem to understand that economic growth fueled by profits is much more effective in the endeavor to improve standards of living than redistributing income. The profit motive drives entrepreneurs to risk their time and money to boost productivity and to innovate, with the goal of attracting as many consumers as possible with better and newer products at affordable prices. Without that motive, economic growth, and progress at improving living standards, would grind to a halt. Accordingly, weakening that motive via policies that excessively redistribute income jeopardizes such progress.

Progressives seem to have a cognitive bias that blinds them to this risk. In their push for ever more income redistribution, higher taxes, and more regulation on businesses, they jeopardize the profit motive of entrepreneurs. Progressives often vilify entrepreneurs as "robber barons."[1] In fact, the entrepreneur is the golden goose that lays the golden eggs. Collectively, entrepreneurs, driven by the profit motive, are the ultimate source of prosperity that benefits everyone. Kill their profit motive, their entrepreneurial spirit, and their work ethic, and you'll kill the golden goose.

In Praise of Progressives

This book is dedicated to progressives. I couldn't have written it without them. I hope they will read it. Any explicit or implicit criticism is offered in the spirit of helping progressives reach a more balanced view of the problems they bring to light and the cures they champion.

In 1509, Desiderius Erasmus of Rotterdam wrote his famous essay titled *In Praise of Folly*. It is a satirical attack on superstitions. Folly is often based on fallacious beliefs. In this essay, I will show that many of the progressives' beliefs and their policy proposals are based on faulty assumptions that are simply not supported by lots of easily available data.

Progressives no doubt mean well. They are always finding income and wealth inequality and recommending policies to fix these problems. In many ways, they succeeded with their New Deal, Great Society, and Obamacare. However, "mission accomplished" is not part of their lexicon.

Progressives are big supporters of big government. Few of them are big fans of capitalism and free markets. But they all believe that government intervention is often necessary to, in essence, "save capitalism" when free markets fail to fairly distribute income and wealth. Government regulation is also required to protect workers and consumers from the excesses of laissez faire capitalism, they say.

Some progressives are outright opponents of capitalism. The moderates among them tend to be socialists. They favor heavy government regulation and supervision of private enterprises and high taxes on the wealthy. The extremists are communists, who oppose private property and champion the nationalization of businesses, especially big ones. This book isn't written for the extremists. It is written for progressives who advocate more government intervention. My goal is to explain what I see as the errors of their ways and the unintended consequences of their policies.

I hope to convince progressives that they must be mindful of the profit motive as a key driver of productivity and prosperity. They can redistribute income with their progressive policies, but aggregate income won't grow if they place too many hurdles in the way of profits.

For those of you who don't need to be convinced about the importance of profits in stimulating productivity and prosperity, I hope that the following analysis will provide you with a better analytical understanding of why our perspective makes the most sense.

Finally, to bridge the gap between "us" and "them," I will acknowledge that progressives have some legitimate current concerns that should be addressed. In particular, shareholder capitalism needs to be reformed so that corporate governance isn't corrupted by crony capitalists, as most clearly evidenced by the excessive pay packages received by some CEOs.

Furthermore, our country clearly faces a child- and elder-care crisis. Many families with one parent working and the other staying home to attend to the needs of family members can barely make ends meet. Many families with two income earners aren't making enough to cover the costs of such care without remaining impoverished. Progressives have been pushing for solutions to both problems. I agree with them on the need to address both issues.

Chapter 1

The Prosperity Economy

Entrepreneurial Capitalism

Businesses can be profitable in economic systems that are competitive as well as those that are not. However, profits tend to increase prosperity more broadly in competitive systems than noncompetitive ones. Capitalism comes in two flavors: entrepreneurial capitalism and crony capitalism. The former tends to be highly competitive, the latter, not so much.

In competitive markets, there are no barriers to entry. Ambitious entrepreneurs with access to the right resources can start a business in any industry. In addition, there's no protection from failure. Unprofitable firms restructure their operations, get sold, or go out of business. There are few if any zombies (i.e., living-dead firms that continue to produce even though they are bleeding cash). Such firms tend to go out of business, but can survive for long periods of time if they are beneficiaries of government support, usually because of political cronyism, or easy credit.

In competitive markets, an increase in aggregate demand for any good or service would raise its market price, stimulating more production among current competitors and attracting new market entrants, which, in turn, will have the consequence of bringing prices back down. If demand drops such that losses are incurred, competitors will cut production, with some possibly shutting down if the decline in demand is permanent. New entrants certainly won't be attracted.

Profits are reduced to the lowest level that provides just enough incentive for enough suppliers to stay in business to satisfy demand at the going market price. Consumer welfare is thus maximized. Obviously, there can't be excessive returns to producers in competitive industries. If there are, those returns will be eliminated as new firms flood into the excessively profitable businesses. Firms that try to increase their profits by raising prices while competitors adhere to the market price will lose market share and eventually go out of business.

Competition is inherently deflationary. No one can raise their price in a competitive market because it is determined by the intersection of aggregate supply and demand. However, anyone can lower their price if they can cut their costs by boosting productivity.

The best way to cut costs and boost productivity is with technological innovations. Companies that can innovate on a regular basis ahead of their competitors can cut their prices, gain market share, and be consistently more profitable than their competitors. Firms that do so gain a competitive advantage that confers a higher profit margin for a while. That's especially true if their advantage is sufficiently significant to put competitors out of business. However, some of their competitors undoubtedly will innovate as well, and there always seem to be new entrants arriving on the scene with innovations that pose unexpected challenges to the established players. In other words, technology is inherently disruptive and deflationary since there is a tremendous incentive to use it to lower costs across a wide range of businesses.

Economists haven't paid enough attention to the impact of technology on the economy. Technology-enabled disruption means that existing business models are being supplanted by new models that bring more efficiency to the production,

That's the theory. In practice, this process doesn't happen rapidly enough, for an obvious reason: Such restructuring is painful. While there are many more winners than losers overall, knowing this doesn't make it easier on the losers. Politicians intervene to reduce the pain with policies aimed at preserving jobs and protecting industries, thus slowing, or even arresting, the pace of progress. The results of such political intervention in the markets are likely to be excess capacity, deflation, and economic stagnation. Opportunities to increase the standard of living for everyone are lost because of political meddling in markets. The politicians claim that their latest round of supportive policies is necessary to fix "market failure," when in fact their previous round of policies kept the markets from doing their job efficiently.

Central bankers often respond to the sting of creative destruction by providing easy credit conditions to alleviate the pain. They hope that lower interest rates will revive demand enough to absorb all the supply and buy time for the losers to become competitive again. It's debatable whether in the past this do-gooder approach has eased the pain or just prolonged it. In my opinion, after the financial crisis of 2008, ultra-easy monetary policies may very well have propped up supply much more than they boosted demand. Credit crunches are nature's way of cleaning out insolvent borrowers from the economy. Easier credit will keep zombie companies in business, which is deflationary and reduces profitability for well-run competitors.

Crony Capitalism

The capitalist system I just outlined is driven by entrepreneurs and needs to be distinguished from the one corrupted by cronyism. "Entrepreneurial capitalism" increases the standard of living better than any other economic system. It is also the most moral economic system. "Crony capitalism" is just one of many variations of corruption. I've long contended that there are only two economic systems: entrepreneurial capitalism and corruption.

Sadly, entrepreneurial capitalism has gotten a bad rap ever since 1776. Perversely, that's when Adam Smith, the great proponent of capitalism, published *The Wealth of Nations*. He made a huge mistake when he argued that capitalism is driven by self-interest. Marketing capitalism as a system based on selfishness wasn't smart. Then again, Smith was a professor, with no actual experience as an entrepreneur.

Smith famously wrote: "It is not from the benevolence of the butcher, the brewer, or the baker that we expect our dinner, but from their regard to their own interest. We address ourselves not to their humanity but to their self-love, and never talk to them of our own necessities, but of their advantages."[2]

This oft-quoted statement is totally wrong, with all due respect to the great professor. The butcher, the brewer, and the baker get up early in the morning and work all day long, trying to give their customers the best meat, ale, and bread at the lowest possible prices. They don't do so because of their self-love, but rather because of their insecurity. If they don't rise and shine early each day, their competitors will, and put them out of business. Entrepreneurial capitalism is therefore the most moral, honest, altruistic economic system of them all. Among its mottos are: "The customer is always right," "Everyday low prices," and "Satisfaction guaranteed or your money back."

The problems start when the butchers, brewers, and bakers form trade associations to stifle competition, or join existing ones that do so. The associations support politicians and hire lobbyists who promise to regulate their industry—for example, by requiring government inspection and licensing. In this way, they raise anticompetitive barriers to entry into their businesses. In other words, capitalism starts to morph into corruption when "special interest groups" try to rig the market through political influence. These groups are totally selfish in promoting the interests of their members rather than their members' customers. At least Smith got that concept right when he also famously wrote, "People of the same trade seldom meet together, even for merriment and diversion, but the conversation ends in a conspiracy against the public, or in some contrivance to raise prices."[3]

Successful entrepreneurial capitalists become crony capitalists when they pay off politicians and hire lobbyists to impose legal and regulatory barriers to market entry to keep out new competitors. It doesn't seem to matter to them that they themselves succeeded because there were no such barriers or because they found ways around any barriers. Rather than cherish and protect the capitalist system that allowed them to succeed, they cherish and protect the businesses that they have built.

Crony capitalism tends to flourish in political and economic regimes that are socialist. Socialism is unambiguously bad for entrepreneurial capitalism, but it provides fertile ground for crony capitalism—that is, if it doesn't lead to communism. Under socialism, private property remains mostly private. Under communism, there is no private property; everything is owned by the state. In either system, the government gets bigger. Under socialism, the ruling regime enacts more laws and regulations that force businesses to manage their affairs increasingly to satisfy their socialist political overseers rather than their capitalist shareholders.

In other words, making deals with the government matters as much as, or more than, competing fair and square in the market for the sole benefit of consumers. That's the fundamental nature of crony capitalism. Businesses become bigger and more politicized as the government gets bigger and more radicalized.

The bottom line on the bottom line is that companies can be profitable in all sorts of economic systems. They can even be profitable in a communist system where the government is the one and only shareholder. However, the profit motive is Adam Smith's "invisible hand" that increases the wealth of a nation much more rapidly and distributes the wealth much more equitably in a competitive system than in a noncompetitive one.

To reiterate, this happens not because of selfishness, as Adam Smith implied, but rather insecurity. Entrepreneurial capitalists are driven to satisfy their customers' needs. That means providing them with the best goods and services at the lowest possible prices, while still making enough profit to stay in business. They know that if they can't do so, they'll lose their customers to competitors who can. Entrepreneurial capitalists are always at risk of going out of business if they don't do right by their customers. They must constantly be thinking about their customers' needs.

Entrepreneurial capitalists do hope to strike it rich. But those who succeed don't do so by being selfish. They do so by coming up with better goods and services that increase the well-being of their customers and attract more of them. Crony capitalists are selfish. They form associations and hire lobbyists and lawyers to protect their businesses from upstart competitors. Political power is an important part of their business model. Buying political influence matters more to them than winning the game in a competitive market with a level playing field.

Chapter 2
The Profits Cycle

Business-Cycle Models

Profits make the wheels of the business cycle go round and round. Over the years, I've come to believe that the profits cycle drives the business cycle. Causality works both ways, of course. However, my simple thesis is that profitable companies expand their payrolls and capacity, while unprofitable companies struggle to stay in business by cutting their costs. They do so by reducing their payrolls and their spending on new equipment and structures to revive their profitability.

In my dramatization of the business cycle, profits are the lead actor on stage in every scene, greatly affecting the performances of all the supporting actors. In the scripts written by most macroeconomists, profits either play only a bit part or never show up at all, like the absent central character in Samuel Beckett's absurdist play *Waiting for Godot*.

One of the pioneers in the study of business cycles was Wesley Clair Mitchell, an American economist. He was also one of the founders in 1920 of the National Bureau of Economic Research, where he was director of research until 1945. Mitchell's magnum opus, *Business Cycles*, appeared in 1913. It analyzed "the complicated processes by which seasons of business prosperity, crisis, depression, and revival come about in the modern world." The focus was on the business cycles since 1890 in the United States, England, Germany, and France. In the first chapter, Mitchell reviewed 13 theories of the business cycle. He wrote

that "all are plausible." He then proceeded to provide an empirical, statistical approach that dispensed with theoretical models.

Today, there is no shortage of theoretical models of the business cycle.

Keynesian macroeconomists tend to focus on the demand
side of the economy. Their models are built on a core assumption that economic downturns are caused by insufficient private-sector demand that needs to be offset by government stimulus. Keynesians prefer more government spending over tax
cuts, figuring that a portion of people's tax windfalls is likely to
be saved rather than spent. They rarely consider the possibility that demand might be weak because government regulations
and policies are depressing profits. All they know for sure is
that they can help with stimulative fiscal and monetary policies.
Keynesians, such as Treasury Secretary Janet Yellen, are firmly in
control in the Biden administration.

Monetarists focus on the money supply. They tend to blame
central bankers for causing the business cycle, and they believe
that announcing and sticking to a reasonable growth rate of the
money supply should reduce economic fluctuations and keep
inflation low and stable. The most celebrated proponent of
this policy was the late American economist Milton Friedman.
However, monetarists lost most of their influence after former
Fed chair Paul Volcker gave their approach a try from October
1979 to October 1982, then abandoned it.

Supply-side economics was very much in fashion during
the Reagan years. Supply-siders prefer to focus on the supply
side rather than the demand side or monetary side of the economy. They believe that the best way to get out of recessions
and to boost economic growth is by cutting marginal tax rates
on both individual and corporate incomes. They also favor
deregulation. I'm inclined to agree with them that reducing

the government-imposed costs of doing business, especially for small companies, is fundamentally good for profits and the economy. American economist Arthur Laffer's thesis that lower tax rates can generate more revenues for the government by stimulating growth also makes sense to me. Supply-siders made a brief comeback during the four years of the Trump administration following their heyday during the Reagan administration.

The Austrian school of thought—launched in the late 19th century by Austrian economist Carl Menger and others—maintains that excessively easy monetary policy creates too much credit during booms. The borrowing binge funds too many dodgy and speculative investments that mostly end badly. Recessions are the inevitable consequence of such unwise policymaking and are necessary to clean out the excesses. These "debt-siders," as I call them, mostly favor reducing the government's meddling in the economy.

Other economists who don't subscribe to the Austrian school also have focused on the financial channel as an amplifier of the business cycle—for example, Yale Professor Irving Fisher. Fisher is remembered for making perhaps the worst stock market call in history: During October 1929, he declared that stocks had reached a "permanently high plateau." He lost a personal fortune as a result. Perhaps to make sense of it all, Fisher wrote a 1933 *Econometrica* article titled "The Debt-Deflation Theory of Great Depressions."[4] The thinking goes: Debt can spiral out of control during recessions, turning them into depressions as both incomes and asset values fall. Debt burdens soar. Bad debts mount. Banks stop lending, forcing asset sales that drive prices lower.

A 1994 paper co-authored by former Federal Reserve Chair Ben Bernanke, who was a Princeton professor at the time, updated Fisher's debt-deflation death spiral, concluding, "Adverse shocks to the economy may be amplified by worsening cred-it-market conditions." Bernanke and his co-authors called this phenomenon the "financial accelerator."[5] It was a bit ironic that in a June 15, 2007 speech, when he was Fed chair, Bernanke updated this analysis just as the accelerator was about to propel the economy off a cliff, à la the final scene of the movie *Thelma and Louise* (1991).[6]

"Minsky Moment" is a term coined in 1998 by PIMCO's chief economist Paul McCulley. Hyman Minsky, a professor of eco-nomics at Washington University in St. Louis, noted that during long periods of economic stability, financial excesses increase until they eventually cause instability. The Minsky Moment is that point when instability begins.

Finally, there have been lots of debates between the New Keynesian economists and the New Classical economists; the latter group includes proponents of the real business-cycle the-ory, which holds that business cycles are neither bad nor good but efficient, and are the result of technological disruptions, not monetary shocks or changes in expectations. They've mostly fought over issues such as rational expectations, price and wage stickiness, and market failure.

Which best fits my thinking among these various schools? The answer is none of the above, since schools of thought tend to promote doctrinaire thinking, often causing the proponents of their doctrines to seek out empirical evidence to prove their point while ignoring any evidence that contradicts their theory.

Admittedly, I am a bit of a puritan about recessions. I agree with the debt-siders, who believe we tend to sin during eco-nomic booms by speculating too much with too much borrowed money. Recessions are nature's way of knocking some sense back into our heads, though the process can be very painful for those who lose their jobs, see their businesses implode, or otherwise experience a significant reversal of fortune. Such punishment is a necessary part of the business-cycle morality play. Booms are followed by busts. That's the natural course.

I agree that some of the sinning during booms often can be blamed on the central bankers. I also agree that soaring credit facilitates the booms that turn to busts. Credit is a better measure of these excesses than are money-supply measures, which tend to have a less stable relationship with the economy. Credit measures also can pinpoint the epicenter of the excesses and predict where the damage will be greatest when the speculative bubble bursts. I think that consumers, investors, and business managers behave rationally most of the time but behave irrationally on a regular basis. They tend to be rational during and after recessions. They tend to lose their minds during booms.

Profits Drive Prosperity

Perhaps I've been biased by my Wall Street background to focus on profits as the main driver of the business cycle. However, in my career I have seen profitable companies consistently respond to their success by hiring more workers, building more plants, and spending more on equipment as well as on R&D. I've seen plenty of unprofitable companies batten down the hatches. They freeze hiring and fire whomever they can ideally without jeopardizing their business. They restructure their operations to reduce their costs, including divesting or shuttering divisions that are particularly unprofitable. They freeze or slash capital budgets.

Notwithstanding politicians' claims, it is profitable businesses that create jobs, not US Presidents or Washington's policymakers and their economic advisers. To be more exact, over the long haul, most of the jobs in our economy are created by small businesses started and run by entrepreneurs that grow into bigger companies. No matter their size, companies behave the same way over the course of the profits cycle. When their profits are growing, they expand their operations. When their profits are falling, they cut back as best they can.

Let's review some evidence to support this simple hypothesis.

The monthly survey of small business by the National Federation of Independent Business shows a very high correlation between the percentage of small business owners who expect to increase employment and the percentage of them saying that their earnings have been higher rather than lower over the past three months (Fig. 1). Their net earnings response is also very highly correlated with the percentage "planning a capital expenditure over the next three to six months" (Fig. 2).

After-tax corporate profits is a data series included with Gross Domestic Product (GDP) in the quarterly National Income and Product Accounts (NIPA). Significantly, its peaks tend to lead the peaks in the business cycle, while its troughs tend to coincide with the troughs in the business cycle (Fig. 3). Nonfarm payroll employment excluding government employment is highly correlated with after-tax corporate profits. That's consistent with my simple "theory" that profitable companies hire, while unprofitable ones fire. Of course, profits are also affected by employment, which drives consumer spending on the goods and services that companies sell.

S&P 500 forward earnings is the time-weighted average of the consensus of industry analysts' estimates of earnings for the current year and next year. It tends to be a very good leading indicator of actual S&P 500 earnings (Fig. 4).[7] The yearly percent change in this series is highly correlated with the comparable growth rates in the aggregate weekly hours of production and nonsupervisory employees as well as capital spending in real GDP (Fig. 5 and Fig. 6).

In other words, there is lots of evidence supporting my thesis that the profits cycle drives the business cycle. Fortunately, recessions tend to be infrequent and short. They are followed by recoveries and relatively long periods of expansions to new record highs in GDP. Indeed, recessionary quarters accounted for just 15% of all the quarters from 1948 through 2020. The average duration of the recessions since 1948 has been 10 months, with the shortest lasting two months (peak to trough), from February through April 2020, and the longest lasting 18 months, from December 2007 through June 2009.

The underlying driver of this prosperity has been the uptrend in profits.

One final related thought before we dive into an analysis of profits in the next chapter. The latest (19th) edition of *Economics* (2010) by Paul Samuelson and William Nordhaus teaches students that economics "is the study of how societies use scarce resources to produce valuable goods and services and distribute them among different individuals." This definition hasn't changed since the first edition of this classic textbook was published in 1948.

I've learned that economics isn't a zero-sum game as that definition implies. Economics is about using technology to increase everyone's standard of living. Technological innovations are driven by the profits that can be earned by solving the problems posed by scarce resources. Free markets provide the profit incentive to motivate innovators to solve this problem. As they do so, consumers get better products often at lower prices. The market distributes the resulting benefits to all consumers. From my perspective, economics is about creating and spreading abundance, not about distributing scarcity.

Chapter 3

What's Wrong with This Picture?

Two Flavors of Profits

Just as significant as the confusion about the role that profits play in our economy is the lack of understanding of the relationship of the various measures of profits and what each includes.

In *S&P 500 Earnings, Valuation, and the Pandemic* (2020), Joe Abbott and I focused on the earnings data relevant to the S&P 500 companies and to forecasting the outlook for the S&P 500 stock price index.[8] These series include quarterly reported and operating earnings as well as dividends. Most of our analysis in that study was based on weekly and monthly series for consensus analysts' expectations for S&P 500 revenues and earnings. We explained why we favor using "forward revenues" and "forward earnings" when we forecast the S&P 500; these are the time-weighted averages of the relevant consensus expectations for the current year and next year. (See that study's Appendix 2: S&P 500 Price Index, Revenues & Earnings Data Series.[9])

In this study, I mostly focus on quarterly profits data for all corporations. The Bureau of Economic Analysis (BEA) compiles the National Income and Product Accounts (NIPA), which include GDP and its components. The BEA reports a preliminary estimate of corporate profits in the second revision of the latest quarterly GDP. This measure of profits is revised when the third revision of GDP is provided. The NIPA measure of profits comes in two flavors:

- *Book profits.* NIPA "book profits" is based on the results reported by corporations on a tax-reporting basis (Fig. 7). It is the difference between the revenues earned and costs incurred in the process of producing goods and services. It excludes dividend income, capital gains and losses, and other financial flows and adjustments, such as deductions for bad debt. That's why the NIPA measure did not show the large run-up in S&P 500 profits during the late 1990s that was primarily attributable to capital gains.

  Corporations consist of all entities required to file federal corporate tax returns, including mutual financial institutions and cooperatives subject to federal income tax; nonprofit organizations that primarily serve business; Federal Reserve banks; and federally sponsored credit agencies. Most corporations report profits on both a financial accounting and a tax accounting basis. The former is based on Generally Accepted Accounting Principles (GAAP) and is provided in reports to shareholders, creditors, and government regulators.

  The BEA's estimates of book profits are primarily based on tax-return information provided by the Internal Revenue Service (IRS) in *Statistics of Income: Corporation Income Tax Returns.* The BEA prefers that source to financial accounting information, as it's more consistent with the NIPA's focus on current production. In financial accounting, corporations sometimes record the value of extraordinary losses before they incur the expenses associated with the losses. However, financial-accounting information is timelier than the tax-return data, so the BEA uses it to derive estimates for the most recent year and for the current year's quarters, making adjustments to conform to tax accounting.

- *Profits from current production.* The BEA's preferred measure of corporate profits is "profits from current production." It is book profits adjusted to restate the historical-cost basis used in profits tax accounting for inventory withdrawals and depreciation to the current-cost measures used in GDP. It is necessary to make these adjustments to calculate corporate profits' contribution to GDP and to the share of National Income, as well as to calculate corporate cash flow. Indeed, I often refer to this concept as "cash-flow profits."

In "Chapter 13: Corporate Profits" of the *NIPA Handbook: Concepts and Methods of the U.S. National Income and Product Accounts*, the BEA explains that the Inventory Valuation Adjustment (IVA) "converts the business-accounting valuation of withdrawals from inventory, which is based on a mixture of historical and current costs, to a current-cost basis by removing the capital gain-like or the capital-loss-like element that results from valuing these withdrawals at prices of earlier periods."[10]

Similarly, the Capital Consumption Adjustment (CCAdj) "converts valuations of depreciation that are based on a mixture of service lives and depreciation patterns specified in the tax code to valuations that are based on uniform service lives and empirically based depreciation patterns." Like the IVA, the CCAdj "converts the measures of depreciation to a current-cost basis by removing from profits the capital-gain-like or capital-loss-like element that arises from valuing the depreciation of fixed assets at the prices of earlier periods."

So corporate profits from current production is equal to book profits plus the IVA and the CCAdj. Both are relatively small adjustments compared to book profits (Fig. 8). Tables 1 and 2 summarize these concepts.

Table 1: Corporate Profits

Corporate "book" profits before tax
> *Plus:* Inventory Valuation Adjustment (IVA)
> *Plus:* Capital Consumption Adjustment (CCAdj)

Equals: Profits before tax from "current production"
> *Less:* Taxes on corporate income

Equals: Profits after tax from "current production"
> *Less:* Net dividends

Equals: Undistributed profits with IVA & CCAdj
> *Plus:* Consumption of fixed capital

Equals: Net cash flow with IVA & CCAdj

Source: Bureau of Economic Analysis, National Income and Product Accounts.

Table 2: Definitions of NIPA Capital & Inventory Adjustments

Capital consumption adjustment (CCAdj)

The adjustment used to convert measures of depreciation that are based on historical-cost accounting—such as the capital consumption allowances reported on tax returns—to NIPA measures of private consumption of fixed capital that are based on current cost with consistent service lives and with empirically based depreciation schedules.

Capital consumption allowances (CCA)

Consists largely of tax-return-based depreciation charges for corporations and for nonfarm proprietorships and partnerships and of historical-cost depreciation charges (calculated by BEA) for farm proprietorships and partnerships, rental income of persons, and nonprofit institutions.

(continued)

Consumption of fixed capital (CFC)

Economic depreciation—that is, the decline in the value of the stock of fixed assets due to physical deterioration, normal obsolescence, and accidental damage except that caused by a catastrophic event. For nonprofit institutions serving households and for general government, CFC serves as a measure of the value of the capital services of the fixed assets owned and used by these entities.

Depreciation

The decline in the value of fixed assets due to physical deterioration, normal obsolescence, or accidental damage. In business accounting, depreciation is generally measured at historical cost, whereas in the NIPAs, the economic measure of depreciation, "consumption of fixed capital," is measured at current cost.

Inventory Valuation Adjustment (IVA)

An adjustment that is made to the NIPA estimates of change in private inventories and of corporate profits and proprietors' income so that they are valued consistently in current prices. The IVA accounts for the difference between the acquisition and the withdrawal value of inventories in certain methods of business accounting, which may arise when the price of a good changes while the good is held in inventory. A negative (positive) IVA represents gains (losses) to the business that are attributable to holding inventories rather than to current production. A corresponding adjustment is made to the estimates of corporate profits and of proprietors' income so that these incomes are associated with current production.

Source: Bureau of Economic Analysis, National Income and Product Accounts.

Contradictory Profits Data

The stock market's permabears were right: NIPA's after-tax book profits series had been flat around $1.8 trillion, at a seasonally adjusted annual rate (saar), from 2012 through the end of 2019 (Fig. 9). That was a remarkably persistent flat trend that certainly didn't seem to justify the bull market in stocks that started in 2009 and continued throughout that period. By the way, the observation also refutes the progressives' claim that the compensation of workers has stagnated because shareholders have benefitted at the expense of workers. That charge doesn't make much sense if profits have also been stagnating.

This just creates more confusion to clear up, which I intend to do.

More recently, the pandemic caused after-tax book profits to drop 19.7% from the fourth quarter of 2019 through the second quarter of 2020 because of the recession caused by the lockdown restrictions during March and April. The measure then rebounded 69.3% through the second quarter of 2021 to a new record high of $2.7 trillion.

Another seemingly bearish anomaly had been that the NIPA measures of the corporate profit margin rose to cyclical and record highs early on during the recovery from the Great Recession of 2008–2009 (Fig. 10). These margins are typically shown as the ratios of either after-tax book profits or after-tax cash-flow profits to nominal GDP. The former peaked at a record high of 11.7% during the first quarter of 2012. It then trended lower to 8.1% during the second quarter of 2020 before rebounding to a new record high of 11.8% during the second quarter of 2021.

In the past, this and other measures of the profit margin tended to reach their cyclical peaks during mid-cycles, when economic expansions typically turned into booms. By then, the previous recession was largely forgotten, and most businesses were doing so well that they started to expand their payrolls and capacity more rapidly and less cautiously. As costs rose faster than revenues, profit margins got squeezed. It's hard to understand why this development would have occurred so early during the business-cycle expansion prior to the pandemic. It just doesn't make much sense.

In our study of the S&P 500 cited above, Joe Abbott and I observed that this stock market index is driven by the total operating earnings per share of the 500 corporations that it includes. Operating earnings are equal to reported earnings less one-time gains and losses. Before it was hit by the pandemic, this measure of after-tax profits was on a solid uptrend since the start of the bull market in early 2009 through the end of 2019 (Fig. 11). From the first quarter of 2012 through the fourth quarter of 2019, it was up 71%. It then plunged during the first half of 2020, but fully recovered by the fourth quarter of that year and rose to new record highs during the first and second quarters of 2021.

The naysayers counter that's because corporate managers have been buying back their shares during most of the bull market since 2009, inflating earnings per share at the expense of their workers and the long-term health of their companies. The problem with this complaint is that it isn't supported by the data, as Joe and I thoroughly explained in our 2019 study titled *Stock Buybacks: The True Story*.[11] As we observed, "There wasn't much difference between the growth rates of S&P 500 earnings on a per-share basis and in aggregate. Surely if corporations were buying back their shares to the tune of several hundred billion dollars per year, the former should grow measurably faster than the latter." We explained that a significant portion of the buybacks have been aimed at offsetting earnings dilution from stocks issued through employee stock-compensation plans.

S&P 500 share buybacks totaled $5.0 trillion from 2011 through 2019. Yet over this same period, the spread between the annual growth rates of S&P 500 per-share and aggregate earnings averaged just 1.0% (Fig. 12 and Fig. 13).

In any event, the bottom line on the bottom line is that S&P 500 aggregate after-tax reported income was on an uptrend from the first quarter of 2012 through the fourth quarter of 2019, rising 58%, while NIPA after-tax book profits rose by 4.4% (Fig. 14).

The S&P 500 profit margin data also tell a more bullish tale than the NIPA margins. Before the pandemic, the S&P 500 operating profit margin rose to peak at a record high of 12.5% during the third quarter of 2018, unlike the NIPA profit margin, which peaked much earlier during the previous business cycle (Fig. 15). Of course, the cut in the corporate tax rate at the start of 2018 boosted the margin, but it was already at a record high of 10.9% during the fourth quarter of 2017. The S&P 500 operating profit margin fell to 8.9% during the second quarter of 2020 because of the lockdown recession, well above the 2.4% low during the fourth quarter of 2008. After the pandemic, it jumped to a record-high 14.0% during the second quarter of 2021.

Before I clear up the confusion, let me add to it some more. The share of National Income attributable to pre-tax corporate profits from current production has been extremely volatile since the start of the data in 1948 (Fig. 16). It is very procyclical, rising sharply during economic expansions and plunging during recessions. Prior to the pandemic, progressives looked past this volatility and discerned a secular uptrend in profits' share of National Income since the start of the 1990s. They detected an offsetting downtrend in the National Income share of the compensation of all employees (Fig. 17). In their opinion, this was indisputable proof that corporations had gained National Income share at the expense of their workers. During 2020 and early 2021, the

National Income share of compensation was extremely volatile, but seemed to be extending a recovery that started in 2015.

If your head is spinning, welcome to my world. All too often, politicians and their economic advisers start with their preconceived notions and search for data that support their biases. Their heads never spin, since they ignore or tune out data that conflict with and challenge their narrative. To avoid this all-too-common bias and to resolve the confusion discussed above, let's take a deeper dive into the data and objectively base our conclusions on what we find.

Chapter 4
Ins and Outs of Profits

ABCs of Corporations

Before we dive much deeper into the data, let's review what is included in NIPA profits. Economists tend to focus their attention on the NIPA profits series while mostly ignoring the S&P 500 profits measure. That's because the NIPA series is more comprehensive. It includes the profits of all corporations, not just those in the S&P 500. Nevertheless, the NIPA and S&P 500 series can provide inconsistent pictures of profits, as we noted above in comparing the trends and profit margins of the two in recent years.

Also as noted above, the NIPA measure comes in two varieties, i.e., book profits and profits from current production. S&P 500 quarterly profits data also come in two flavors, i.e., reported and operating. While the latter excludes net write-offs, it is never adjusted to derive a current production measure like NIPA's cash-flow profits. The NIPA series isn't adjusted for net write-offs to derive an operating version of NIPA profits. Therefore, I believe that it makes the most sense to compare S&P 500 reported earnings to NIPA book profits, both on a pre-tax basis and using four-quarter sums to smooth out seasonality (Fig. 18).

Since 1993, aggregate S&P 500 reported profits has tended to average around 60% of NIPA corporate profits (Fig. 19). Where does the other 40% of NIPA profits come from? The answer is the other 6.8 million or so corporations in the US. That was the number of companies that filed tax returns with the IRS for 2020.

(See Appendix Table 1.) So while the 500 corporations in the S&P 500 account for about 60% of NIPA profits, their number is tiny compared to 6.8 million corporations that account for the rest of NIPA profits. NIPA profits includes both C corporations and S corporations:

- *C corporations.* The C corporation gets its name from Subchapter C of the Internal Revenue Code. The IRS explains that the profit of a C corporation "is taxed to the corporation when earned, and then is taxed to the shareholders when distributed as dividends. This creates a double tax. The corporation does not get a tax deduction when it distributes dividends to shareholders. Shareholders cannot deduct any loss of the corporation."[12] The S&P 500 companies are all C corporations, with their shares publicly traded.

- *S corporations.* S corporations are so named because they are taxed under Subchapter S of the Internal Revenue Code. On its website, the IRS explains that S corporations elect to pass corporate income, losses, deductions, and credits through to their shareholders for federal tax purposes. Shareholders of S corporations report the pass-through of income and losses on their personal tax returns and are assessed tax at their individual income tax rates. This allows S corporations to avoid double taxation on the corporate income.[13] They are not publicly traded.

According to the *NIPA Handbook*, corporate profits includes all US public and private C and S corporations.[14] As noted earlier, it also includes other organizations that do not file federal corporate tax returns—such as certain mutual financial institutions and cooperatives, nonprofits that primarily serve business,

Federal Reserve banks, and federally sponsored credit agencies. Much of the difference between the NIPA measure of profits and the S&P measure is attributable to S corporations and other C corporations that are not in the S&P 500.

The IRS rules limit the number of shareholders of an S corporation to no more than 100, who may be individuals, certain trusts, and estates. They may not be partnerships, corporations, or non-resident alien shareholders. The S corporations must be domestic and have only one class of stock. They cannot be certain financial institutions, insurance companies, and domestic international sales corporations.[15]

S corporations were added to the Internal Revenue Code by the Technical Amendments Act of 1958. The IRS Statistics of Income (SOI) has always included them as part of total corporations. This is the aggregation that comprises the base of NIPA corporate profits.

S corporations report on a separate tax form, the 1120-S, which has existed since the addition of S corporations in 1958 and originally was very similar to the standard corporation Form 1120. However, with the passage of The Tax Reform Act of 1986, Form 1120-S underwent a major overhaul. Beginning in 1987, several income and expense measures were removed from page 1 of the form, to be passed directly through to shareholders via Schedule K. The changes made Form 1120-S similar in this respect to the partnership tax return Form 1065.

In the early 1980s, C corporations produced almost all business income. By 2013, only 44% of business owners' income was earned through C corporations. Now the percentage is about half, with owners of S corporations and other pass-through businesses earning the other half. The shift occurred because of the tax and legal changes that benefitted pass-through business owners and made the pass-through form more attractive to file. For instance, in 1986, the top individual income tax rate fell below the corporate tax rate. This created significant incentives for a business to unincorporate and for new businesses to organize as pass-throughs.[16]

The IRS reports that there were 5.0 million S corporations in the United States in 2020—almost three times the number of C corporations (Fig. 20). (See Appendix Table 1.) The BEA notes on its website:

> S corporations are legal entities that pay no Federal corporate profits taxes; instead, all of their earnings are treated as taxable income of shareholders, regardless of whether the income is distributed as dividends or retained by the corporation. As a result, most income is paid out as dividends. Since 1998, S corporation dividends generally represented 82 to 92 percent of the profits of S corporations that reported gains. When losses are included, dividends accounted for more than 100 percent of net S corporation profits for most years during that period.[17]

Again, S corporations allow their shareholders to avoid the double taxation of income, first at the corporate level, then on the dividends paid out by the corporation. As a result, most of the income of S corporations is paid out as dividends. Since S corporations tend to distribute most of their earnings to their limited number of shareholders as dividends, which are then taxed as personal income, they boost corporate profits even though they directly benefit the income of owners of the S corporations who receive dividends and are taxed on them.

This helps to explain why NIPA's effective corporate tax rate has been well below the statutory rate (Fig. 21). To reiterate, S corporations' profits are in the NIPA measure, but their profits are taxed as dividends in personal income. The effective corporate tax rate of the S&P 500 has also been below the statutory rate, but not by as much (Fig. 22).

Accounting for S Corporations

Let's have a closer look at S corporations since they represent a significant portion of NIPA profits. Their existence seems to be unknown to many economists, who must be assuming that NIPA profits is simply a more comprehensive measure of profits than is the aggregate earnings of the S&P 500. S corporations are hiding in plain sight. After all, there are millions more of them than the 500 C corporations in the S&P 500.

We can use available data on dividends to get some insights on the importance of S corporations to total dividends and, therefore, to total profits. The NIPA accounts include dividends paid by all corporations in both the quarterly table for corporate profits and in the monthly table for personal income (Fig. 23). The two series are nearly identical. The BEA's website explains:

> "Net dividends" is shown in several NIPA tables that present estimates of corporate profits. Net dividends is measured as gross dividends paid by US corporations in cash or other assets, plus US receipts of dividends from the rest of the world, net of dividend payments to the rest of the world, less dividends received by US corporations. This measure of net dividends represents the net dividend income of US residents arising from their ownership, in whole or in part, of US and foreign corporations.

Furthermore:

> "Personal dividend" income is shown in NIPA tables that present estimates of personal income and is defined as the dividend income of persons from all sources. It equals net dividends paid by corporations less dividends received by federal, state and local governments. Pension funds, some

insurance reserves, and private trust funds are considered
to be the property of persons, so dividends received by
these institutions are included in personal dividend income.
Dividends received by mutual funds are generally redistrib-
uted to the mutual fund shareholders, so these dividends
can be considered to "pass through" to their owners and are
also included in personal dividend income.[18]

In addition to annual and quarterly data for the dividends paid
by all corporations (including both C and S corporations), there
are annual and quarterly data series for dividends paid by the
S&P 500 since the fourth quarter of 1926. Furthermore, the IRS
compiles an annual series for dividends paid by S corporations,
which is currently available from 1991 through 2017 (Fig. 24).[19]

The S&P 500 accounted for 35.9% of all dividends during
2020, down from a high of 40.8% during 1992 (Fig. 25). S corporations accounted for only 18.2% of total dividends in 1991. That
percentage rose to a record high for the series of 45.6% during
2001. On average, S corporations accounted for around 41% of
total dividends from 2001-2017.

New Profits Data

Just by coincidence, as I was researching the available data on S
corporations discussed above, the BEA was doing the same. On
May 17, 2021, the BEA posted a report titled "Prototype NIPA
Estimates of Profits for S Corporations."[20] The abstract summa-
rizes the goal of the report:

> Currently in the NIPAs, all corporate profits are combined
> with no separate distinction for C corporations and S corpo-
> rations, but taxes on corporate profits only represent taxes
> paid by C corporations. This paper proposes a methodology
> for splitting NIPA profits before taxes (PBT), corporate taxes,
> and dividends between S corporations and C corporations.

NIPA Table 7.16, "Relation of Corporate Profits, Taxes, and Dividends in the National Income and Product Accounts to Corresponding Measures as Published by the Internal Revenue Service," provides a walkthrough of IRS data to NIPA estimates of corporate profits, taxes, and dividends. We use this same framework to estimate S corporations. We first identify the items that are relevant to S corporations, then determine the methodology for separately estimating the S corporation portion.

The NIPA report found that S corporations' share of total corporate receipts less deductions rose from 23% in 2012 to 31% in 2017, an increase of 8 percentage points. Their share of total NIPA profits before taxes with IVA and CCAdj increased from 27.2% in 2012 to 35.3% in 2017 (Fig. 26 and Fig. 27). (See Appendix Table 2.) S corporation dividends as a share of total national dividends has remained close to 39% from 2012 through 2017, according to the report. (See Appendix Table 3.) S corporations have tended to distribute about two-thirds of their pre-tax profits as dividends, while the S&P 500 corporations have tended to distribute about 40% of their after-tax reported profits as dividends in recent years (Fig. 28). (See Appendix Table 4.)

The S Class

This raises an interesting question: Which class are the owners of S corporations in? Progressives undoubtedly throw them into the capitalist class. After all, they all own their incorporated businesses, and they employ workers. The NIPA report cited above shows that in 2017, the 1.6 million C corporations employed 55.9 million workers with an annual payroll of $3.5 trillion, while the 4.7 million S corporations employed 34.6 million workers with an annual payroll of $1.5 trillion.

On the other hand, the owners of S corporations certainly work long hours since the success or failure of their business is mostly up to them. The IRS and NIPA treat the owners of S corporations as individual income taxpayers, just like every other working stiff.

This suggests that S corporations have had a significant impact on exaggerating the increase in corporate profits' share of National Income over this period. Obviously, I am implying that S corporation dividends are more like labor compensation than profits. Excluding these dividends from profits shows that this adjusted measure's share of National Income has been significantly lower than the all-inclusive measure of profits (Fig. 29 and Fig. 30). The flip side of this story is that labor's share of National Income is higher if we treat dividends paid by S corporations as labor income (Fig. 31 and Fig. 32).

The plot thickens when we investigate the impact of other pass-through businesses on National Income. Before we go there, Table 3 below reviews the concept of National Income and its distribution.

A Nation of Proprietors

S corporations are one of three main types of pass-through businesses. The other two are sole proprietorships and partnerships. Sole proprietorships are incorporated businesses owned by single persons, who fill out Schedule C (Profits or Loss from Business) in Form 1040 of their individual income tax returns. A partnership is like a sole proprietorship in function but allows for the association between two or more persons who agree to combine their resources and skills for a mutual profit (and loss). Pass-through businesses do not pay taxes at the business level. Instead, profits or losses are passed through to the owners and partners and are taxed at individual income tax rates. In the NIPA measure, their income is not included in corporate profits, but rather as proprietors' income in personal income.

Table 3: GDP, GNP, and National Income

Gross Domestic Product

> *Plus:* Income receipts from the rest of the world
>
> *Less:* Income payments to the rest of the world

Equals: Gross National Product

> *Less:* Consumption of fixed capital
>
> *Less:* Statistical discrepancy

Equals: National Income

> Compensation of employees
>
> Wages and salaries
>
> Supplements to wages and salaries
>
> Proprietors' income*
>
> Corporate profits*
>
> Rental income of persons**
>
> Net interest and miscellaneous payments
>
> Taxes on production and imports less subsidies
>
> Business current transfer payments (net)
>
> Current surplus of government enterprises

Addendum:

> Gross Domestic Income equals National Income plus consumption of fixed capital***

* With inventory valuation and capital consumption adjustments.
** With the capital consumption adjustment.
*** Consumption of fixed capital (i.e., economic depreciation) equals capital consumption allowances (i.e., tax-reported depreciation) plus the capital consumption adjustment.
Source: Bureau of Economic Analysis.

Pass-through businesses are the dominant business type in the United States, and their number has steadily increased relative to C corporations in recent years. From 1997 through 2018, the number of C corporations edged down from 2.2 million to 2.1 million. Over this same period, the number of S corporations doubled from 2.5 million to 5.1 million, and the number of sole proprietorships and partnerships increased from 17.2 million to 27.1 million. In total, there were 36.2 million pass-through businesses in 2018, up from 21.5 million during 1997, and 17 times the number of C corporations (Fig. 33). (See Appendix Table 1.)

As discussed earlier, one explanation for this growth in pass-through businesses is that the US tax code taxes C corporations more heavily than pass-through businesses. C corporations are taxed twice—once at the entity level by the corporate income tax and once at the shareholder level when profits are distributed as dividends or stockholders realize capital gains. Pass-through businesses, however, are taxed only once, under the individual income tax, meaning they are not subject to any business-level tax. Following the 1986 federal tax reform, which dramatically cut individual income tax rates, pass-throughs became much more attactive business structures.

Despite their heavier tax burdens and fewer numbers than pass-through businesses, C corporations still generate more business revenue. In 2015, C corporations accounted for fewer than 5% of all business tax returns but generated more than 60% of all business revenue. Pass-throughs accounted for more than 95% of all returns but less than 40% of all business revenue. Though C corporations earn the lion's share of revenue, pass-through businesses surpass C corporations when it comes to net income. In 2015, pass-through businesses accounted for 63.3% of net business income compared to 36.7% for C corporations (Fig. 34).[21]

The bottom line is that both pass-through businesses and C corporations contribute importantly to the American economy: C corporations, relatively few in number but high in net income per entity, contribute hefty revenue generation, while pass-through businesses generate nearly three-fifths of the nation's net business income (Fig. 35).

As previously noted, S corporations' profits are included in NIPA's measure of total corporate profits, and the dividends they pay out are included in personal income along with the dividends paid by C corporations. What about proprietorships and partnerships? Their profits are included in the proprietors' income component of personal income. The *NIPA Handbook's* Chapter 11 defines this concept as follows:

> Nonfarm proprietors' income measures the income, before deducting income taxes, of sole proprietorships, partnerships, and other private nonfarm businesses that are organized for profit but that are not classified as corporations. Sole proprietorships are businesses owned by a single individual. Partnerships include most associations of two or more of: individuals, corporations, noncorporate organizations that are organized for profit, or of other private businesses. Other private businesses are made up of tax-exempt cooperatives, including credit unions, mutual insurance companies, and rural utilities providing utility services and farm marketing and purchasing services.[22]

This raises the same interesting question as raised by S corporations. Which class should include proprietors? Are they capitalists or are they workers? Progressives view them as capitalists because they own their own businesses and employ workers. But proprietors are also employees of their firms, and their incomes are typically more exposed to the ups and downs of their businesses than the incomes of their steadily paid employees. Again, in 2018, there were 27.1 million proprietorships and 4.0 million partnerships. If the former employed only one person and the latter employed only two persons, that would add up to 34.9 million workers, or 23% of the household measure of employment during 2017.[23]

In fact, the IRS data show that the number of partners in the 4.0 million partnerships totaled 27.4 million in 2018. (See Appendix Table 1.) So the number of pass-through business owners and partners totaled 54.5 million. That puts the number of pass-through business owners and partners up 21.1 million, or 63.2%, from 33.4 million during 1997.

Admittedly, these numbers are inflated by partnerships that are limited liability companies (LLCs). LLCs have limited liability (like corporations), but they may be taxed as pass-throughs. During 2017, only 8% of sole proprietorship returns indicated status as LLCs. That same year, LLCs accounted for 69% of partnerships.

Real estate and rental and leasing accounted for about half of partnerships and nearly a third of all partners. Many of the partners are investors rather than employees in the LLCs.

Nevertheless, just the sum of S corporations and sole proprietorships increased 59% from 20.3 million in 1999 to 32.2 million in 2018. These figures strongly suggest that the US continues to evolve into a nation of more and more entrepreneurial proprietors.

Proprietors' income on a pre-tax basis has been equivalent to about 80% of pre-tax corporate profits since the 1960s (Fig. 36 and Fig. 37). Proprietors' share of National Income declined from about 16% in the late 1940s to 7% in the early 1980s (Fig. 38). It has been on a gradual uptrend since then, though mostly stable around 9% since 2000. Progressives undoubtedly would be inclined to add proprietors' income to profits share, while conservatives would be more inclined to add it to the share of compensation of employees (Fig. 39 and Fig. 40). I am in the latter camp.

The remarkable proliferation of pass-through businesses in the United States suggests that the distinction between employers and employees isn't as rigid as it has been in the past. Clearly, more and more Americans are running their own businesses, providing employment for themselves and for others. They have a lot of skin in the game. If their businesses fail, they also lose their jobs along with their employees. They are likely to know their employees personally and have lots of incentive to keep them happy. In turn, most of their employees are likely to want to do whatever they can to make the business successful, knowing that it is small and more exposed to competitive pressures than are most large corporations.

In my opinion, the BEA's data that has been so widely used to track the National Income shares of workers versus producers is seriously flawed. A possible patch would be to treat the pass-through income of S corporations, proprietorships, and partnerships more as labor income than as profits.

Chapter 5
Uses and Alleged Abuses of Profits

Cash Flow and Capital Spending

Corporate profits have gotten most of the attention in my analysis so far. Rightly so, since their role as the key driver of productivity and prosperity is widely ignored. Profits are the golden eggs laid by the golden goose, i.e., corporate America. Yet they represent a relatively small portion of corporate cash flow.

In the NIPA, corporate cash flow is equal to "undistributed profits with inventory valuation and capital consumption adjustments" plus "consumption of fixed capital," i.e., economic depreciation. Undistributed profits equals after-tax corporate profits from current production less dividends (Fig. 41 and Fig. 42). Depreciation is an expense item on corporate income statements that is subtracted from revenues to reflect the cost of replacing capital assets over time. In a sense, it is a tax shelter since it reduces taxable profits but still is available as cash for a company to use for operating purposes and for capital spending.

So, for example, during 2020, pre-tax corporate profits totaled $2,244 billion. Taxes reduced that by $276 billion, resulting in after-tax profits of $1,968 billion. Dividends totaled $1,395 billion, leaving $573 billion in undistributed profits. Adding back depreciation of $1,957 billion resulted in cash flow of $2,330. So undistributed profits accounted for just 23% of cash flow. Since the mid-1980s, undistributed profits has fluctuated around 25% of corporate cash flow (Fig. 43).

Corporations can supplement their cash flow by borrowing from banks and in the corporate bond market. They can also issue stock. Data available for all corporations show that they raised $2,398 billion in the bond market and $335 billion in the stock market during 2020 (Fig. 44). Both are record highs; however, they are gross rather than net amounts. Of course, corporations also have cash sitting on their balance sheets.

What did corporate managements do with all their cash flow? NIPA provides data on total "nonresidential fixed investment," i.e., capital spending by all businesses, not just corporations. During 2020, this item totaled $2,800 billion, and it rose to a record high of $3,030 billion (saar) during the second quarter of 2021. The NIPA cash flow of just corporations was $2,339 billion during 2020.

The Fed's data for nonfinancial corporations show that they had cash flow of $2,025 billion and spent $2,029 billion during 2020 on fixed investment (Fig. 45). In the past, their capital spending typically tended to match their cash flow.

The Fed also has a data series for business fixed investment by nonfinancial noncorporate entities that includes the capital spending of all the proprietorships and partnerships in the nonfinancial business sector. The sum of the Fed's two series for capital spending by nonfinancial corporations and nonfinancial noncorporate entities is almost identical to the BEA's series for total nonresidential fixed investment in nominal GDP (Fig. 46). Capital spending by the latter group of businesses has fluctuated around 11% of the total since the early 1990s (Fig. 47).

My conclusion is that profits and proprietors' income are the key drivers of the economy. On a pre-tax basis, they reached a record high of $4.1 trillion during the first quarter of 2021. There is no evidence to support the progressives' claim that the managements of C corporations haven't spent enough on fixed investment. All the measures of capital spending mentioned above rose to record highs in early 2021.

The True Story About Stock Buybacks

In recent years, progressive politicians have railed against corporate stock buybacks. They see buybacks as a major cause of income and wealth inequality, deficient capital spending, and lackluster productivity. In their opinion, buybacks have contributed greatly to the stagnation of the living standards of most Americans in recent years. Therefore, they want to limit buybacks or even ban them.

In a February 3, 2019 *New York Times* op-ed, Senators Chuck Schumer (D-NY) and Bernie Sanders (D-VT) claimed that our nation's glory days can be restored by limiting corporate stock buybacks.[24] According to the two senators, the period from the 1950s through the 1970s was a golden age for workers because "American corporations shared a belief that they had a duty not only to their shareholders but to their workers, their communities and the country that created the economic conditions and legal protections for them to thrive."

However, in recent decades, corporate managements and their boards of directors have become greedy, the narrative goes, focusing on maximizing "shareholders' earnings" at the expense of workers' earnings. The result has been the "worst level of income inequality in decades," the two progressive senators claimed.

As proof, they offered the "explosion of stock buybacks." From 2008 through 2017, corporations had boosted their earnings per share and the value of their stocks by spending close to 100% of their profits on buybacks (53%) and dividends (40%)—which the senators characterized as corporate "self-indulgence."

They bemoaned that corporations haven't been investing enough to strengthen their businesses or boost the productivity of their workers. So, they claimed, stock-holding managements have gotten richer at the expense of workers who don't hold stock and haven't benefitted from rising stock prices—thus exacerbating both income and wealth inequality. Adding insult to injury, "the median wages of average workers have remained relatively stagnant." According to the two progressive senators, the corporate fat cats have gotten fatter on buybacks while workers "get handed a pink slip."

In our 2019 study titled *Stock Buybacks: The True Story*, Joe Abbott and I disputed this narrative promoted by progressives.[25] We concluded, "The true story is hiding in plain sight." We observed many of the S&P 500 companies buy back their shares to offset the increase in the number of shares outstanding that results when employee compensation takes the form of stock options and stock grants that vest over time, not just for top executives but for many other employees. In effect, the ultimate source of funds for such stock buybacks is the employee compensation expense item on corporate income statements, not profits and not bond issuance as the progressives contend.

The Senators also argued that buybacks and dividends have accounted for almost all after-tax corporate profits, implying that the funds could have been better spent on boosting their workers' pay and on capital spending to boost productivity. They seem to be unaware that undistributed after-tax corporate profits are a small percentage of cash flow, and that cash flow has been quite enough to fund plenty of capital spending.

As I observed in the Introduction, the widely believed notion that buybacks boost earnings per share by reducing the share count isn't supported by the data Standard & Poor's provides for the S&P 500 companies. While S&P 500 companies repurchased a whopping $5.0 trillion of their shares from the first quarter of 2011 through the fourth quarter of 2019, the average annual spread between the growth rates in S&P 500 earnings per share and aggregate S&P 500 earnings has been tiny, i.e., just 1.0% over this period. One explanation for this surprising development is that many S&P 500 companies repurchase their shares to offset the increase in the number of shares outstanding that results from compensation paid in the form of stock.

It's not just top executives who are compensated in company stock but other employees as well. However, there isn't much data to assess how many workers participate in stock compensation plans. The website of the National Center for Employee Ownership Data notes that the quadrennial General Social Survey (GSS) has been asking respondents if they get stock options at work since 2002. The post states: "Looking just at applicable respondents, those who report working for a for-profit company (excludes non-profit and government workers), 22% say they 'own any shares of stock in the company where you now work, either directly or through some type of retirement or stock plan.'"[26]

Buybacks are not solely used "to return cash to shareholders," as commonly believed. While dividends are paid directly to shareholders, buybacks don't directly benefit investors if they simply result in equities being purchased in the open market to offset stocks distributed to employees. Those shifts from unconstrained sellers to constrained buyers (who can't sell until their stock grants vest) arguably have a net bullish impact that indirectly benefits all investors.

Buybacks shouldn't be compared to profits. The cost of buying back shares for the purpose of offsetting the obligations of employee stock grants is reflected for repurchasers in the compensation-related expense in calculating profits.

A February 2008 *BEA Briefing* titled "Employee Stock Options and the National Economic Accounts" reported: "In December 2004, the Financial Accounting Standards Board (FASB) issued a new standard—FAS-123R—for companies that requires them to value employee stock options . . . using a fair-value-based method at the time they are granted and to record this value on financial reports as a compensation expense over the period of vesting."[27]

A March 2011 *BEA Briefing* titled "Comparing NIPA Profits with S&P 500 Profits" observed: "NIPA accounting and tax accounting have always treated employee stock options as an expense only when (and if) options are exercised. It is an operating expense and therefore always a cost deduction in the NIPA profits calculation."[28] Before the FASB standard became effective for calendar-year companies on January 1, 2006, "GAAP option expense reporting was completely at a company's discretion and reported as a nonoperating expense or, often, not reported at all. Since 2006, options grant expense was mandated by GAAP. It was included in the Standard & Poor's reporting starting in 2006 as an operating profits deduction."

So: It makes no sense to compare the total amount that S&P 500 corporations spend on buybacks to their after-tax profits, as is often done! In the NIPA, money spent on buybacks to cover employee stock plan obligations doesn't come out of the after-tax profits pool as dividend payouts and capital outlays do. The contention that money used for buybacks would be better invested in growth of the business is specious. In the NIPA measure, dividend distributions, on the other hand, do come out of after-tax profits, leaving undistributed profits. These undistributed profits, along with cash flow from the depreciation allowance, can be spent on capital outlays. The cost of the buybacks that are turned around as stock compensation to employees is reflected in the income statement as an expense.

So why is the S&P 500 stock price index highly correlated with buybacks (Fig. 48)? Some progressives claim that this proves that buybacks are in fact driving the stock market. The coincident relationship between the S&P 500 stock price index and buybacks reflects that compensation—with some percentage paid in stock—rises in a growing economy. If stock-based compensation rises, buybacks tend to do so as well. So economic growth drives both buybacks and the stock market. That's why they move in sync. It's not that buybacks drive the stock market, as widely believed.

University of Massachusetts Professor William Lazonick authored a very influential article in the September 2014 *Harvard Business Review* titled "Profits Without Prosperity."[29] He has been quoted by progressives who want to put a lid on buybacks. The professor called for "an end to open-market buybacks." In Lazonick's opinion, trillions of dollars have been spent to artificially boost earnings per share by lowering the share count. The money should have been used to invest in the capital and labor of corporations to make them more productive, he contended. He seemed to be under the impression that buybacks and dividends have been absorbing nearly 100% of earnings, leaving nothing for capital spending.

That seems to be arithmetically correct. But it is simply wrong. The problem is the claim's underlying assumption that the biggest source of corporate cash flow is profits; rather, it is depreciation allowances. They reflect the expenses incurred when companies have to replace depreciating assets. They boost corporate income because they reduce companies' tax bill, since depreciation is sheltered from taxation.

To repeat, buybacks that are offsetting stock compensation aren't financed with cash flow. The source of funds is the substitution of non-cash, stock-based compensation to employees that would otherwise be paid in cash.

Finally, blaming buybacks for widespread income stagnation doesn't make any sense. The data I review in the next chapter clearly show that standards of living have been rising in record-high territory for most Americans for several years, contrary to the progressives' tale of widespread woe.

Chapter 6
Productivity and Prosperity

The Productivity-Pay Gap Myth

On Thursday, May 27, 2021, President Joe Biden lashed out at critics of his economic stimulus plans. He flatly rejected the notion that his policies were causing problems in the labor market. Earlier that year, in a February 4 *Washington Post* op-ed, economist Larry Summers, who was the US Treasury Secretary in the Clinton administration from 1999 to 2001, trashed Biden's American Rescue Plan.[30] He said it was too stimulative and too inflationary and included overly generous unemployment benefits that would disincentivize the unemployed from seeking work.

The plan was enacted on March 11 and included $300 per week in federal supplemental unemployment benefits through September 6. There was mounting evidence during the spring of 2021 that Summers might have been right: The federal jobless benefits included in the Act seemed to be providing a disincentive to work. For example, during June, the number of job openings rose to a record high of 10.1 million, exceeding the 9.5 million unemployed workers during the month. Initial unemployment claims remained stubbornly high through July.

On Friday, May 7, the US Chamber of Commerce issued a statement calling on Congress to cancel the extra weekly federal unemployment benefits, citing worker shortages. It claimed that the benefit "results in approximately one in four recipients taking home more in unemployment than they earned working."[31]

By early June, 25 state governors traced their states' labor shortages to federal unemployment benefits and eliminated these benefits in their states.

In effect, Biden countered that if employers paid their workers more, they would find more of them.[32] "When it comes to the economy we're building, rising wages aren't a bug, they're a feature," he said. He went on to renew his call for Congress to raise the federal minimum wage to $15 an hour. "A lot of companies have done extremely well in this crisis, and good for them," he said. "The simple fact is, though, corporate profits are the highest they've been in decades. Workers' pay is at the lowest it's been in 70 years. We have more than ample room to raise worker pay without raising customer prices."

According to this logic, profits are too high because businesses aren't paying their workers enough. The tune may change, but the woeful refrain of this progressives' song never does.

Like most past presidents, Biden has claimed that his policies create jobs. "We've had record job creation, we're seeing record economic growth, we're creating a new paradigm. One that rewards work—the working people in this nation, not just those at the top." Unlike most past presidents, Biden also seems to believe that the government can implement policies that will boost wages.

Biden might be right about that to the extent that employers have been forced to offer higher wages to compete with generous unemployment benefits. He may or may not succeed in raising the minimum wage by law. He certainly is one of the most pro-labor presidents since Franklin Delano Roosevelt.

In any case, the goal of any president should be to increase workers' standards of living by increasing their purchasing power. That can happen only if nominal wages rise faster than consumer prices. And that can happen only if productivity rises, because real wages are determined by productivity, not by politicians or unions. However, politicians and unions often create impediments that weigh on productivity and boost labor costs. The result can be a wage-price spiral, with prices rising faster than wages.

The government's attempts to lift wages can backfire. The unintended consequence of such political intrusions into the labor market could be that real wages decline along with productivity.

In a market economy, competitive forces tend to cause labor's inflation-adjusted pay to be commensurate with marginal productivity. The motto of many labor organizers in the past and now is "A fair day's wage for a fair day's work." A competitive economy tends to make that ideal happen. This is one of the classic and time-tested insights of microeconomic analysis.

The most widely followed measure of productivity is the ratio of real output to hours worked in the nonfarm business sector, which is reported on a quarterly basis (with monthly revisions) by the Bureau of Labor Statistics (BLS) in the *Productivity and Costs* release.[33] It is often compared to the release's time series on nonfarm business real hourly compensation (RHC). Here is how the BLS defines hourly compensation in the "technical notes" of the release:[34]

> The measure includes accrued wages and salaries, supplements, employer contributions to employee benefit plans, and taxes. Estimates of labor compensation by major sector, required for measures of hourly compensation and unit labor costs, are based primarily on employee compensation data from the NIPA, prepared by the BEA. The compensation of employees in general government, nonprofit institutions and private households are subtracted from compensation of employees in domestic industries to derive

employee compensation for the business sector. The labor
compensation of proprietors cannot be explicitly identified
and must be estimated. This is done by assuming that proprietors have the same hourly compensation as employees
in the same sector. The quarterly labor productivity and
cost measures do not contain estimates of compensation for
unpaid family workers.

It has been widely asserted by progressive politicians (and the
liberal economists they rely on) that a gap between productivity
and real hourly compensation has been widening since the mid-
1970s (Fig. 49). This myth has been promoted by the Economic
Policy Institute (EPI) in Washington, DC for a long time.

The EPI's website states that the "nonprofit, nonpartisan
think tank" was created in 1986 "to include the needs of low-
and middle-income workers in economic policy discussions. EPI
believes every working person deserves a good job with fair pay,
affordable health care, and retirement security."[35]

That's certainly a worthy goal, topping many a partisan
progressive organization's agenda. However, all too often, these
organizations seize upon misleading data to support their case
for new policies. They are never satisfied with what they have
already accomplished. Progressives are ever looking to make
progress toward their goals, while conservatives are ever trying
to slow them down.

The EPI's website brags that "[i]n the 1990s EPI researchers were the first to illustrate the decoupling of productivity and
pay in the U.S. economy, a trend now widely recognized as a
key element of growing economic inequality."[36] This claim was
most recently updated by the EPI in a May 2021 post titled "The
Productivity-Pay Gap." It features a compelling chart showing
that inflation-adjusted hourly compensation tracked productivity very closely from the late 1940s through the 1960s. But since

the 1970s, the former has lagged the latter, resulting in a widening gap between the two. The conclusion is obviously disturbing: "This means that although Americans are working more productively than ever, the fruits of their labors have primarily accrued to those at the top and to corporate profits, especially in recent years." The EPI explains:

> Rising productivity provides the potential for substantial growth in the pay for the vast majority. However, this potential has been squandered in recent decades. The income, wages, and wealth generated over the last four decades have failed to "trickle down" to the vast majority largely because policy choices made on behalf of those with the most income, wealth, and power have exacerbated inequality. In essence, rising inequality has prevented potential pay growth from translating into actual pay growth for most workers. The result has been wage stagnation.[37]

Not surprisingly given the EPI's partisan approach to research, their supporting data are seriously flawed. They continue to make a rookie mistake: using the wrong price deflator to adjust hourly compensation. They use the Consumer Price Index (CPI), long recognized as upwardly biased; doing so weighs misleadingly on real hourly compensation, creating a totally bogus gap! To be fair, they are following the misleading lead of the BLS, which releases the productivity and compensation data in its quarterly report and also adjusts hourly earnings by the CPI.

The productivity-pay gap is a myth based on RHC data derived using the CPI. The gap narrows significantly using the personal consumption expenditures deflator (PCE deflator), which is widely recognized as a more accurate measure of consumer prices (Fig. 50).[38] The gap almost disappears using the nonfarm business price deflator (NFB deflator), which is also reported in the BLS's *Productivity and Costs* release.

It makes much more sense to divide hourly compensation by the NFB deflator than by the CPI or even the PCE deflator. That's because the NFB deflator is the measure of prices received by employers when they calculate the labor costs associated with producing more product. Workers' purchasing power obviously depends on the prices of items such as food, gasoline, and rent. But in a competitive market economy, employers pay for a fair day's work, not for the cost of living.

The data confirm the microeconomic theory that the real value of labor is determined by productivity. The 20-quarter percentage change, at an annual rate, in real hourly compensation based on the NFB deflator has been tracking the comparable growth rate in productivity very closely since the start of the data in 1952 (Fig. 51). The same can be said using the PCE deflator to derive RHC (Fig. 52).

Productivity growth has tended to have decade-long cycles. It was very strong during the late 1940s through the early 1950s, during the 1960s, and during the second half of the 1990s through the first half of the 2000s. Those were glory days for the growth rate in real hourly compensation as well.

The most notable two periods of weakness in the growth rate of productivity were from the first quarter of 1966, when it peaked at a record 4.6%, through the third quarter of 1982, when it fell to 0.2%. During the second period of significant weakness, it fell from 4.0% through the fourth quarter of 2003 to bottom at 0.6% through the fourth quarter of 2015. The declines in the growth rate of RHC during those two periods closely tracked the declines in the comparable growth rates of productivity. Since around 2015, both have been growing at faster and faster paces.

The Wage Stagnation Myth

The data clearly belie the productivity-pay gap claim often made by progressives. Also not supported by the data is their related claim that workers' pay has stagnated for decades, including President Biden's bizarre statement that wages are the lowest in 70 years. He obviously misspoke and must have known that doesn't make much sense. Nevertheless, wage stagnation remains a widely believed myth among progressives and others.

An extremely flawed August 2018 study by the Pew Research Center concluded that Americans' purchasing power, based on the CPI-adjusted average hourly earnings (AHE), has barely budged in 40 years![39] In fact, using the PCE deflator, it has been rising since 1995 at a solid average annual rate of 1.5%.

In an April 19, 2019 op-ed for *The New York Times* titled "Progressive Capitalism Is Not an Oxymoron," Joseph Stiglitz lamented: "Despite the lowest unemployment rates since the late 1960s, the American economy is failing its citizens. Some 90 percent have seen their incomes stagnate or decline in the past 30 years."[40] He should know, since he won the 2001 Nobel Prize in Economics. That is, he should know better!

In fact, all the major measures of real hourly compensation were either at or near recent record highs during the second quarter of 2021 (Fig. 53 and Fig. 54). That's true whether we use the NFB deflator or the PCE deflator. The pandemic might have distorted the data, but all the major measures of inflation-adjusted hourly pay were at record highs during the fourth quarter of 2019, before the pandemic started.

A couple of the measures did stagnate during the 1980s through the mid-1990s, but they've all been rising since then. Here are their total and average annual increases from the first quarter of 1995 through second quarter of 2021 using the PCE deflator rather than the more theoretically pure NFB deflator: nonfarm business hourly compensation (54%, 2.1%); Employment Cost Index including wages, salaries, and benefits (29%, 1.1%); and AHE for production and nonsupervisory workers (38%, 1.5%) (Fig. 55).

To be fair and balanced, the first two measures of real hourly pay may be boosted by high-income earners. However, the real AHE series applies only to production and nonsupervisory workers, who account for about 80% of payroll employment (Fig. 56). It has been increasing 1.5% per year on average since 1995. There certainly has been no stagnation in this measure of real pay.

Median real household income, the annual series compiled by the Census Bureau and used to measure poverty in America, has been a big favorite of economic pessimists and political progressives in recent years because it confirmed their view that most Americans' standard of living has stagnated for years.

My view long has been that lots of other, more reliable indicators of income confirm that most Americans' standard of living has been improving for many years. Now even the Census series confirms my story. So, it's back on the right track after misleadingly showing stagnation from 2000 through 2016 (Fig. 57).

After remaining flat over that period, the median household series, which Census adjusts for inflation using the CPI, is up 9.2% from 2016 through 2019 and hit new highs during each of the last three years (2017–2019). Also up over the past three years to new record highs are the CPI-adjusted Census series for median family (up 11.0%), mean household (10.7%), and mean family (12.5%) incomes. During 2019, most Americans were better off than ever before.

Again, the rookie mistake is using the CPI rather than the PCE deflator to adjust for inflation. From 1995 through 2019, median household income deflated by the CPI is up 24.4%, while it is up 36.0% divided by the PCE deflator (Fig. 58).[41]

The Census data still have lots of other issues. Most importantly, they are based on surveys asking a sample of respondents for the amount of their money income before taxes. So Medicare, Medicaid, food stamps, and other noncash government benefits—which are included in the personal income series compiled by the BEA—are excluded from the Census series. Furthermore, the BEA data are based on "hard" data like monthly payroll employment statistics and tax returns. The BEA also compiles an after-tax personal income series reflecting government tax benefits such as the Earned Income Tax Credit.

The BEA series for personal income, disposable personal income, and personal consumption expenditures—on a per-household basis and adjusted for inflation using the PCE deflator rather than the CPI—all strongly refute the stagnation claims of pessimists and progressives (Fig. 59 and Fig. 60). These series have all been on solid uptrends for many years, including from 2000 through 2019, rising 32.5%, 35.4%, and 32.6%, respectively, over this period, often to new record highs. There was no stagnation whatsoever according to these data series. Conversely, there was lots of growth!

The standard critique of using the BEA data series on a per-household basis is that they are means, not medians. So those at the very top of the income scale, the so-called "One Percent," in theory could be skewing both the aggregate and per-household data. That's possible for personal income but unlikely for average personal consumption per household. The rich can only eat so much more than the rest of us, and there aren't enough of them to substantially skew aggregate and per-household consumption considering that they literally represent only 1% of taxpayers.

The Roaring 2020s?

The 20-quarter annualized growth rate in productivity has rebounded from a recent low of 0.6% during the fourth quarter of 2015 to 2.0% during the second quarter of 2021. In my Roaring 2020s scenario, productivity growth should continue to increase, matching previous cyclical highs of around 4.0% by the middle of the decade. Before I flesh out the happy outlook for the 2020s, allow me to review what happened during the 1970s as a cautionary tale for the remainder of the current decade and to explain why I don't expect a repeat.

Just about everything that could go wrong on the inflation front did so in the 1970s. President Nixon closed the gold window on August 15, 1971. During the decade, the foreign-exchange value of the dollar plunged by 53% relative to the Deutsche mark, and the price of gold soared 1,402%.

The Commodity Research Bureau raw industrials spot price index, which was relatively flat during the 1950s and 1960s, jumped 165% during the decade because of the weaker dollar. A supply shock in late 1972 through early 1973 sent soybean prices soaring. As a result of the oil crises of 1973 and 1979, the price of a barrel of West Texas Intermediate crude oil rose 870% from $3.35 at the start of the decade to $32.50 by the end of the decade. Cost-of-living adjustment clauses in labor union contracts caused these price shocks to be passed through into wages, resulting in an inflationary wage-price spiral.[42]

We can see what happened more clearly by focusing on the 20-quarter percent change, at an annual rate, in nominal hourly compensation, which includes wages, salaries, and benefits. This measure rose from a low of 3.5% through the second quarter of 1965 to a high of 11.4% through the first quarter of 1982. Meanwhile, productivity growth, measured on a comparable basis, dropped from a peak of 4.6% through the first quarter of 1966 to zero through the third quarter of 1982. The 20-quarter annualized growth rate in unit labor costs (ULC), which is the ratio of nominal hourly compensation to productivity, soared from about zero per year during the first five years of the 1960s to over 10.0% during the late 1970s and early 1980s (Fig. 61). Since ULC is the key determinant of consumer price inflation as measured by the 20-quarter annualized percent change in the core PCE deflator, price inflation also soared from the mid-1960s through the early 1980s.

The decade of the 1970s offers the most relevant cautionary tale for current times, with inflationary pressures escalating during 2021.

During the second half of 2020 through the first half of 2021, both food and nonfood commodity prices rose sharply, and the dollar fell. There were mounting signs of labor shortages and upward pressure on wage inflation. Amazon and Walmart announced plans to boost compensation for their workers. On May 18, 2021, Bank of America said that it will raise the hourly minimum wage of its US employees from $20 to $25 by 2025. The bank also required its vendors and suppliers to pay their employees at least $15 an hour, with 99% of vendors already doing so.[43]

Nevertheless, I don't expect a wage-price spiral. I do expect that rising wages will be justified by rising productivity. In my Roaring 2020s scenario, I expect that technology-led productivity growth will offset most of the inflationary cost pressures up ahead. I continue to monitor the 20-quarter percent change in productivity at an annual rate. As noted above, it bottomed most recently at 0.6% during the fourth quarter of 2015. It was up to 2.0% during the second quarter of 2021. In my Roaring 2020s scenario, I think it could match the previous three cyclical peaks of around 4%!

The productivity boom I am anticipating in coming years should be driven by demographic factors that are depressing the growth in the labor force. The response is likely to be a revolution of technological innovations that will augment both the physical and mental productivity of the labor force.

Since the end of World War II, the five-year average annual growth rate in the US civilian population peaked around 2.0% in the late 1950s (Fig. 62). It has been mostly declining ever since to a record low of 0.4% at the end of 2020. The civilian working-age population exceeded the growth rate of the overall population most significantly during the 1970s. The Baby Boomers turned 16 years and older from 1962 to 1980.

As a result, the five-year average annual growth rate in the civilian labor force grew fastest during the 1970s, ranging between 2.5% and 3.0% at an annual rate (Fig. 63). That was attributable to an influx of Baby Boomers into the labor force, with the labor force participation rate of the cohort's women increasing significantly. This growth rate of the civilian labor force has been declining since the early 1980s, falling to a low of just 0.3% through June 2021.

Depressing the growth of the labor force has been mostly negative growth in the portion of the labor force aged 16–24 years old since the mid-1980s (Fig. 64). Offsetting that drag has been a significant increase in the labor force aged 65 years old and older, reflecting the aging of the Baby Boomers who remained in the labor force beyond the traditional retirement age (Fig. 65). However, many of the oldest Boomers are retiring and dropping out of the labor force, adding to the drag on overall labor force growth.

The information technology revolution should boost productivity growth, more than offsetting the slowdown in the labor force. The IT revolution that started in the early 1990s was clunky back then. PCs and even laptops were as big as suitcases. They were very good for word processing and for running spreadsheets but not much else. Cellphones were the size of a brick. Software upgrades had to be installed on each individual digital device, requiring lots of IT people for most companies. Nevertheless, the boom in the output of PCs and telecommunications equipment boosted the productivity of the technology industry during the late 1990s and early 2000s. Demand for such equipment was also boosted by the Y2K problem, causing many businesses to upgrade their IT systems.

By the way, in 1987, economist Robert Solow famously wrote, "You can see the computer age everywhere but in the productivity statistics." His aphorism came to be known as the Solow Productivity Paradox.[44] In fact, back then, computers and information processing equipment were a relatively small share of GDP and of the capital stock. In industries like finance and insurance, where computers were heavily used, output was hard to measure. Computers weren't as productive back during the 1980s and 1990s as they are today. Like the diffusion of electricity during the 1920s, the productivity implications of the new information technologies are showing up now after a long lag.[45]

So, for example, in 2006, Amazon Web Services began offering cloud storage. Ever since, more and more software companies have developed cloud-based programs that can be accessed by digital devices, the new versions of which are automatically available on those devices. There has been a host of other innovations along the way that have made technology more powerful, more useful, and cheaper for just about any business. As a result, integrating these technologies into running almost every business has become an imperative. Companies that don't do so will be crushed by their competitors that do.

In other words, every company today is a tech company. I've often observed that Yardeni Research is a tech company. We've been on the Amazon cloud since 2011. We rent Microsoft Office in the cloud. We recently replaced a patchwork of software programs that we use for production, CRM, and distribution with an integrated platform from HubSpot in the cloud. Our system automatically polls our data vendors' servers for new data, which immediately update the thousands of charts and hundreds of chart books on our website, which resides in the cloud. We've been using Zoom since the start of 2020 to produce video podcasts easily and quickly. We have just one IT consultant, working remotely from Denver. We've all been working from our home offices since 2004.

Even before the Great Virus Crisis (GVC), companies had been moving to incorporate into their businesses a host of state-of-the-art technologies in the areas of quantum computing, 5G telecommunications, robotics, artificial intelligence, 3-D manufacturing, the Internet of Things, and augmented reality, among others. The GVC accelerated that trend as companies scrambled to do business ever more efficiently in the post-pandemic era. In current dollars, capital spending on technology jumped 14.7% on a year-over-year basis during the second quarter of 2021 to another record high (Fig. 66). It accounted for a record 52% of capital spending during the first half of 2021 (Fig. 67).

The Real Phillips Curve

Proponents of the Phillips Curve have long believed that there is an inverse relationship between the unemployment rate and both wage inflation and price inflation. Missing in this very simplistic model of inflation is productivity. A tighter labor market can boost wage inflation, but it also can stimulate productivity. In this scenario, nominal and real wages will rise without putting as much upward pressure on consumer prices. As an alternative model, let's consider my Real Phillips Curve Model, which compares the unemployment rate to the growth rates of both productivity and inflation-adjusted hourly compensation.

With few exceptions, there has been an inverse correlation between the unemployment rate and the growth rate of productivity (using the 20-quarter percent change at an annual rate) (Fig. 68). Productivity growth tends to be best (worst) when the jobless rate is low (high). That makes sense: Unemployment tends to be high during recessions, when weak demand depresses productivity because output falls faster than hours worked.

The 1970s was a decade of relatively high unemployment, resulting in both a sharp drop in productivity growth and a wage-price spiral. I believe that labor will continue to be relatively scarce during the 2020s, which is why I expect a productivity boom over the remainder of the decade, resulting in subdued price inflation.

Interestingly, there is also an inverse correlation between the unemployment rate and inflation-adjusted hourly compensation (Fig. 69). High unemployment depresses real pay because it depresses productivity. Low unemployment boosts productivity, which boosts real pay without boosting consumer price inflation.

I conclude that profit-led prosperity shouldn't be inflationary since it is likely to boost productivity growth. Progressives need to be aware that prosperity resulting from their well-intentioned stimulative fiscal and monetary policies can be inflationary. Inflation is the same as a very regressive tax that hurts low-income households much more than high-income households.

Now let's turn to the relationship between prosperity and income and wealth inequality, as well as income mobility.

Chapter 7

Income and Wealth in America

Prosperity and Inequality

As I observed in the Introduction, entrepreneurial capitalism tends to cause income inequality. Successful entrepreneurs tend to get richer faster than the rest of us, especially during periods of prosperity. So, perversely, times of prosperity tend to increase inequality: The less well-to-do also prosper, but not as much as the rich, so the income and wealth gaps between them widen. On the other hand, during good times, there is also more upward income mobility. The lavish lifestyles of the "rich and famous" are covered by the media and provide progressive politicians with lots of evidence that capitalism worsens inequality. During bad times, everyone is generally worse off than they were during the good times.

Take your pick: Do you prefer a capitalist economic system that provides plenty of upward income mobility along with lots of opportunities and incentives for entrepreneurial capitalists to increase everyone's standards of living but results in more income and wealth inequality? Or do you prefer a more collectivist economic system, such as socialism, that provides a more equitable distribution of income and wealth as a result of more downward economic mobility and with fewer opportunities and incentives for entrepreneurs to improve consumers' standards of living?

It is the profit motive that drives entrepreneurs to innovate. As I explained in Chapter 1, the profit motive drives entrepreneurs to search for new products and services that would benefit the most consumers. In other words, successful entrepreneurial capitalists are first and foremost thinking about their customers, not about themselves. It is the popularity and rapid proliferation of "new, new things" sold by innovators that contribute to widespread increases in standards of living and general prosperity. Entrepreneurs are always worrying that their competitors will put them out of business by offering consumers newer, better, and cheaper products. In this sense, entrepreneurs are driven by insecurity, not by selfishness.

Crony capitalists, on the other hand, are selfish. They tend to collude with their competitors on ways to share their market among themselves while erecting barriers to entry to keep new competitors out of their business. They also spend lots of time figuring out ways to please and work with government officials and regulators rather than consumers. They especially love and promote government regulations that keep competitors out of their market.

In an ideal entrepreneurial capitalist system, everyone has the same opportunity to increase their own income and wealth by enhancing the standards of living of their customers. The incentives to do so increase aggregate prosperity although worsening income inequality. Alternative economic systems tend to produce less inequality but also less prosperity.

But what about the fairness issue? Is it fair that a minority of entrepreneurs invariably earn income and amass wealth well beyond their share of the population? The most successful ones certainly tend to have more money than they can ever hope to spend on trophy properties, cars, and other luxuries. Often, they will invest their windfalls in their own businesses or in new businesses. Their aim is to either expand their initial enterprises or invest in new ones that presumably might also strike it rich by developing beneficial products and services for their customers.

Then again, to be fair, there is always the temptation for successful entrepreneurial capitalists to turn into crony capitalists who use their economic power to stifle competition by currying favor with politicians. Cronies tend to get rich at the expense of consumers. They do so by using their political clout to bury their competitors. Facing less competition, the cronies can charge more for their products and cut corners that reduce their quality.

I will address the crony problem in the next chapter. But first, let's have a closer look at the data relevant for analyzing income and wealth inequality along with the fairness issue. The income data do show income inequality, but they also show that much of it is offset by upward income mobility.

Income Mobility vs Inequality

Progressive economists who claim that income and wealth inequality in America is a pernicious and insidious problem always have data at hand that seem to prove it. They typically compare the current percentages of total income earned and total wealth held by the top 10% of households to the comparable percentages in the past. The current percentages are invariably higher than past ones. They conclude that the government needs to fix this problem by raising income taxes on the rich and even by taxing their wealth, which already has been taxed once, when received as income. They see punitive taxes as the only way to redistribute the "unfair" gains of the rich that presumably came mostly at the expense of everyone else.

The progressive economists rarely consider the possibility that widespread prosperity tends to result in economic inequality, which beats the alternative of greater income equality with less prosperity resulting from higher taxes. Higher taxes reduce the profit motive. It is the profit motive that drives profits, which drive companies to expand their payrolls and capacity, as I discussed in Chapters 1 and 2.

Furthermore, the progressive analysis of income distribution over time fails to consider that widespread upward income and wealth mobility may be distorting their simplistic analysis. They are comparing two static pictures of income distribution at two distinct points in time and failing to see the dynamic action in the film rolling in between their two freeze frames. Along the way, while some of the rich get richer, some of them get poorer. Similarly, some of the poor get poorer, while some of them get richer. On balance, the data strongly suggest that income mobility is to the upside.

While some of the top 10% of households today may also have been in that group, let's say 20 years ago, they undoubtedly have been joined by households that previously had been in the lower economic tiers. The nouveau riche in turn have been replaced in the lower economic tiers by younger households that just recently started earning income and accumulating wealth. Many younger, lower earning, less wealthy households tend to be aspirational, seeking to climb the ladder of success as they age. Many succeed, thanks to the natural process of upward economic mobility in our entrepreneurial capitalist system. Of course, mobility works both ways, as some well-off households experience economic setbacks.

We can analyze income mobility in the United States using the federal income tax return data compiled by the IRS that are available from 2001 through 2018 by brackets for adjusted gross income (AGI).[46] Before we do so, let me share my main finding with you: While total AGI divided by the total number of returns is up considerably, the average AGI per return for each of the five major brackets hasn't changed very much over the seventeen years from 2001 through 2018.

How can that be? How can the macro data show so much prosperity on average for all returns, while the micro data show stagnation in the average AGI per return among each of the five income brackets? The answer is income mobility.

While incomes tend to rise over time for plenty of households within the brackets, the averages for each of the income brackets have been held down by newcomers from the lower tiers. In the case of the lowest tier, the newcomers are mostly younger households just starting to earn income.

That leads to a radically different and more optimistic conclusion about inequality than the one proffered by the progressives' pessimistic narrative. Their comparative static analysis completely ignores the fact that many households are aspirational and want to climb the income ladder to higher tiers. And many of them do so, especially as they get more work experience and get paid more for it.

Most of the households in the top tiers today were in the bottom tiers when they were younger. As they've risen from one tier to the next, or leaped a few, each tier's new members have tended to offset the income gains of the more established households in each tier. But as the number of households in each tier has increased thanks to income mobility, the total AGI for each of the higher tiers has increased too.

Now, let's look at the IRS tax return data that confirm my more optimistic analysis. (See Appendix Table 5.)

The number of returns increased 18.0% from 130.3 million during 2001 to 153.8 million during 2018. Total AGI increased 88.7% from $6.17 trillion to $11.64 trillion over this same period. Average AGI per return increased 59.7% from $47,400 to $75,700.

(See Appendix Table 5, rows 7 and 13.) Over this same period, the PCE deflator rose 36.0%. So inflation-adjusted total AGI increased 38.7%. Inflation-adjusted AGI per return increased 17.4% over this 17-year period, or 1.0% per year on average.

That's yet another real-pay-per-household series discrediting the wage stagnation claim of progressives. Nevertheless, progressives can dispute my assertion by observing that real AGI per return is a mean, not a median, and claim that most of its gains have accrued to the top earners, while the real incomes of workers stagnated. That's their woeful tale, and they're apparently sticking to it!

Again, they are missing the impact of upward income mobility.

To see this, let's dive deeper into the IRS data by comparing the individual returns, the AGI, and the average AGI per return during 2001 and 2018 for each of the five income groups, along with their percentage changes over that period. (See Appendix Table 5.)

Again, the number of returns rose 18.0% over this period. The returns filed by the lowest-income group earning $50,000 or less per year declined 4.1%. This might reflect progressive changes in the tax code that meant that fewer households in this bracket were required to file returns. It could also reflect upward income mobility. The number of returns filed by the four income groups above the lowest group all increased with a collective gain of 72.9%, suggesting plenty of upward income mobility. The same pattern can be discerned in the total AGIs for each of the four top income groups.

Another way to slice and dice the data is to compare the number of returns filed by each AGI group as a percentage of total returns during 2001 and during 2018, then to calculate the changes in these percentages. The percentage of total tax returns filed by the lowest income group dropped from 71.2% to 57.8%, while all the other income groups rose from 28.8% to 42.2%. (See Appendix Table 5, row 19.) These numbers suggest a significant amount of upward income mobility too.

This conclusion isn't supported by the relatively flat *average* AGI per return for each of the five brackets. (See Appendix Table 5, rows 14-18.) However, that doesn't imply income stagnation on an individual household level. As discussed above, various households perpetually move in and out of the various brackets; the brackets experience turnover owing to income mobility. Indeed, almost all the gains in total AGI per income group have been attributable to triple-digit percent increases in the number of households filing returns with AGIs in the top three income ranges.

The IRS data clearly show that it is upward income mobility, not rising average AGIs per income bracket, that has been increasing both nominal and real AGIs. I submit that the data strongly suggest that the AGIs of the great majority of Americans have improved significantly since 2001. Income mobility has lifted many of them into higher income brackets.

This happy development can be explained in part by the huge proliferation of pass-through businesses. As mentioned in Chapter 4, the number of pass-through business enterprises (including S corporations, sole proprietorships, and partnerships) ballooned between 2001 and 2018 by 14.7 million to a total of 36.2 million. The sum of the number of sole proprietors and the number of actual partners in all the partnerships expanded by 21.1 million to 54.5 million. (See Appendix Table 1.) Over the same period, the number of tax returns shot up by 23.5 million to 153.8 million. (See Appendix Table 5, Row 1.) The proliferation of pass-through businesses undoubtedly has been a major contributor to the increase in the number of returns and to upward income mobility.

Progressives look at the same data as I do and see inequality and an increasingly unfair economic system. I look at the data and see rising prosperity that is mostly fairly distributed *over time* through upward income mobility.

A Taxing Fairness Question

Now let's see what the IRS data suggest about the fairness issue with respect to income distribution and taxation. To do so, we can compare the federal income taxes paid by each income group to their AGI, total AGI, and total taxes. (See Appendix Table 6.)

During 2019, Americans filed 153.77 million individual income tax returns for 2018. The income group earning $500,000 or more filed 1.65 million returns for that year, or 1.1% of the total (Fig. 70). During 2018, the "One Percent" had AGI totaling $2.53 trillion, or 21.7% of the $11.64 trillion total (Fig. 71). That year, they paid $639 billion in taxes. That's 25.3% of their AGI. It's also a record 41.5% of all income taxes paid, up from 26.1% in 2001, when the top bracket accounted for only 0.4% of returns (Fig. 72). Meanwhile, the rest of us working stiffs, the "Ninety-Nine Percent" with 78.3% of total AGI, picked up only 58.5% of the total tax bill for 2018, down from 73.9% in tax year 2001. Is that fair?

For 2018, there were 88.93 million tax returns filed by individuals with AGI of $50,000 or less, accounting for 57.8% of returns. They had AGI of $1.76 trillion, or 15.1% of the total. That year, they paid $65 billion in taxes. That's only 3.7% of their AGI and only 4.2% of all income taxes paid, down from 13.9% of all income taxes paid in 2001. Is that unfair?

What should be the fair share for the One Percent? Instead of about 40% of the federal government's tax revenue, should the One Percent be kicking in 50%? Why not 75%? These taxpayers would be less well off, but everyone else would be better off—unless paying more in taxes saps the incentive for entrepreneurs to keep creating new businesses, jobs, and wealth.

By the way, a June 8, 2021 exposé by three reporters at progressive news organization ProPublica uncovered that the rich haven't been paying their fair share of taxes.[47] The present-day muckrakers gained access to "a vast trove of Internal Revenue Service data on the tax returns of thousands of the nation's wealthiest people, covering more than 15 years." The cache included "not just their income and taxes, but also their investments, stock trades, gambling winnings and even the results of audits."

Progressive politicians were outraged, not by the illegality of the leak of confidential tax records of individuals, but by ProPublica's findings. No claim was made that any of the billionaires had done anything illegal, especially since some of them were actually audited. Rather, they were accused of taking advantage of the tax code by finding legitimate ways to lower their tax bills. The goal of ProPublica was to show that the tax code is rigged in favor of the wealthy.

ProPublica's analysis was sensationalist and very misleading. It confused income and wealth. It implied that the rich haven't paid taxes on their unrealized capital gains. The tax code imposes a capital gains tax on *realized* not unrealized gains. Indeed, the report acknowledged that "the skyrocketing value" of assets owned by the ultrarich "are not defined by U.S. laws as taxable income unless and until the billionaires sell."

Another bombshell loophole uncovered by the exposé is that the tax code allows a deduction for a portion of the value of assets with depreciating values from taxable income each year over the useful life of the asset, known as amortization. This is a standard feature of tax systems around the world.

Ironically, some of the billionaires exposed by ProPublica have been major supporters of the progressive agenda for many years including Michael Bloomberg, George Soros, Bill Gates, and Mark Zuckerberg. Here's another scoop: "No one among the 25 wealthiest avoided as much tax as [Warren] Buffett, the grandfatherly centibillionaire. That's perhaps surprising, given his public stance as an advocate of higher taxes for the rich." In addition, a spokesman for Soros said in a statement: "Between 2016 and 2018 George Soros lost money on his investments, therefore he did not owe federal income taxes in those years. Mr. Soros has long supported higher taxes for wealthy Americans." In any event, the accountants working for Soros undoubtedly will continue to find legitimate ways in the tax code to lower his tax bill.

Balance Sheet of Inequality

Now let's turn to wealth inequality from 1989 through early 2021. The bottom line is that wealth inequality has worsened slightly during this period. That's because the major source of wealth inequality is ownership of equity in publicly traded and close-ly-held corporations. Wealth inequality, like income inequality, tends to worsen during periods of prosperity, because strong profits growth increases the market value of corporate equities.

Progressives have had more success in redistributing income than in spreading the wealth. Recently, a few of them have pro-posed imposing a wealth tax. For some of them, redistributing wealth may be too radical since it threatens the sanctity of pri-vate property. Wealth taxes would certainly amount to a major challenge to the underlying legal foundation of our capitalist economy, raising major issues about the rule of law, the sanctity of contracts, and property rights.

In any event, progressive economists have struggled with their empirical analysis of wealth. Their studies on wealth inequality have been based on flimsy data sets and lots of questionable assumptions.

Meanwhile, a large team of the Fed's researchers have constructed a new database containing quarterly estimates of the distribution of US household wealth since 1989. They launched it with the release of a March 2019 working paper titled "Introducing the Distributional Financial Accounts of the United States."[48] The Distributional Financial Accounts (DFA) is an impressive accomplishment combining quarterly aggregate measures of household wealth from the Financial Accounts of the United States and triennial wealth distribution measures from the Survey of Consumer Finances.

I believe that the new database can be used to resolve most, but not all, of the controversial issues about wealth distribution in the US. The DFA's balance sheet of the household sector is much more comprehensive and timely than previously existing sources.

The Fed's researchers observe that their "approach produces rich and reliable measures of the distribution of the Financial Accounts' household-sector assets and liabilities for each quarter from 1989 to the present." The data can be used to study the distribution of wealth in America by wealth and income percentiles, education, age, generation, and race. This can be done for each of the items listed in the balance sheet of the net worth of the US household sector, shown in Table 4.

Table 4: Household Balance Sheet

Net Worth
 Assets
  Nonfinancial assets
   Real estate
   Consumer durables
  Financial assets
   Checkable deposits and currency
   Time deposits and short-term investments
   Money market fund shares
   Debt securities
    US government and municipal securities
    Corporate and foreign bonds
  Loans
   Other loans and advances
   Mortgages
  Corporate equities and mutual fund shares
  Life insurance reserves
  Pension entitlements
  Equity in noncorporate business
  Miscellaneous assets
 Liabilities
  Loans
   Home mortgages
   Consumer credit
   Depository institutions loans*
   Other loans and advances
  Deferred and unpaid life insurance premiums

*Not elsewhere classified.
Source: Federal Reserve Board, Distributional Financial Accounts (DFAs).

Since the third quarter of 1989 through the first quarter of 2021, the net worth of households has increased 532% to a record $129.5 trillion. (See Appendix Table 7.) The share held by the top 1% of wealthy households rose from 23.4% to 32.1% over this period (Fig. 73). The share held by the top 90%-99% group has been relatively steady between 35.0% and 40.0%. It was 37.7% during the first quarter of 2021. The share held by the 50%-90% group has declined from 35.5% to 28.2% over the period. The bottom 50% had only a 2.0% share of household net worth.

Put more simply, the top 10% held 69.8% of household net worth during the first quarter of 2021, up from 60.8% during the third quarter of 1989. Yes, wealth inequality is significant and has gotten worse.

The top 10% of wealthy households not only have a disproportionately high share of household assets, but also have a very small share of household liabilities. During the first quarter of 2021, they had 64.8% of household assets and only 25.2% of household liabilities (Fig. 74 and Fig. 75).

Much of America's wealth inequality has been attributable to equities. This asset class totaled $37.4 trillion, or 25.7%, of household assets during the first quarter of 2021. The share of corporate equities and mutual funds held by the top 10%, i.e., the wealthiest households, rose from 82.1% in the third quarter of 1989 to 88.7% in the first quarter of 2021 (Fig. 76).

The next biggest asset class in the household sector's balance sheet is real estate, at $33.8 trillion during the first quarter of 2021. Real estate remains among the most equitably distributed assets in America, with the top 10% of households' share at 44.8% and everyone else sharing a collective 55.3% as of the first quarter of 2021 (Fig. 77).

Pension entitlements likewise are relatively equitably distributed; they totaled $29.9 trillion during the first quarter of

2021. The top 1% had only a 5.0% share, while the bottom 50% had only a 3.0% share, but everyone else had a 92% share (Fig. 78).

The Fed's DFA database on household wealth does not include the present discounted value of Social Security benefits provided by the government to American households, especially those that progressives claim are not getting their fair share of household wealth. An August 2, 2021 working paper by five economists from the University of Wisconsin and the Federal Reserve made a very good case for including Social Security in studying the distribution of household wealth inequality and found much less of it as a result![49]

Progressive economists have examined the Fed's DFA and found it wanting as a database for assessing wealth inequality. Furthermore, they question the usefulness of tax data for assessing income inequality. Two of the most influential are Emmanuel Saez and Gabriel Zucman, both professors of economics at the University of California, Berkeley. For many years now, they have been convinced that income and wealth inequality in the United States is pernicious and getting worse. They seek to reverse this trend by providing progressive politicians with as much alarming data as they can find to make their case—and have done so in numerous articles they coauthored. They advised Senator Elizabeth Warren (D-MA) during her 2020 presidential campaign.

Saez and Zucman updated their views in a 2020 working paper titled "The Rise of Income and Wealth Inequality in America: Evidence from Distributional Macroeconomic Accounts."[50] Right off the bat, they wrote, "Between 1978 and 2018, the share of pre-tax income earned by the top 1% rose from 10% to about 19% and the share of wealth owned by the top 0.1% rose from 7% to about 18%." Not once was the phrase "income mobility" mentioned in their paper. They like the concept of the Fed's DFA project but expressed some technical objections. They have no objection to the DFA's omission of Social Security because they don't believe that the programs benefits should be treated as an asset in analyses of wealth distribution. That's perverse since many households view this progressive program as a substitute for accumulating retirement assets.

The two Berkley professors also expressed their reservations about using tax data for analyzing income inequality. They noted the large and growing gap between total personal income and taxable income:

> On the labor side, untaxed labor income includes tax-exempt employment benefits (contributions made by employers to pension plans and to private health insurance), employer payroll taxes, the labor income of non-filers, and unreported labor income due to tax evasion. The fraction of labor income which is taxable has declined from 80–85 percent in the post-World War II decades to just under 70 percent in 2018, due to the rise of employment fringe benefits—in particular the rise of employer contributions for health insurance, particularly expensive in the United States. Most studies of wage inequality ignore fringe benefits even though they are a large and growing fraction of labor costs.

I believe their argument actually supports my side of the story since a few of the components of untaxed labor income are sizeable, and their tax-free status is especially beneficial to households with lower incomes, particularly employer contributions to pension and health insurance plans.

Saez and Zucman also have worked with Thomas Piketty, who wrote a 2014 bestseller titled *Capital in the Twenty-First Century*. The book's central thesis is that inequality is a feature of capitalism that can be reversed only through government intervention. Piketty favors a global tax on wealth.

I disagree.

Bull markets in stocks coincide with periods of prosperity in America when corporate profits are growing solidly. Households with significant holdings of equities in their portfolios see their wealth rise faster than those of households with less significant holdings. As previously noted, entrepreneurs particularly tend to see their incomes rise faster than other people's incomes during these periods as well.

Is this a problem that needs to be fixed? I don't think so.

There's risk in constraining the ability of the wealthy to seize opportunities since that would affect the economic wellbeing of us all. The wealthy tend to diversify their stock market windfalls, benefitting diverse industries. They invest in private equity deals, and they fund startups; the easy availability of capital provides up-and-coming entrepreneurs with the financing they need to fund their ventures, helping them to give it a go.

I conclude that in such ways, our system of entrepreneurial capitalism increases and distributes prosperity faster and better than any other economic system. Income and wealth inequality both increase during prosperous times. That beats the alternative, i.e., bad times for all—which constraining the prosperity-seeding activities of the wealthy would invite. In any event, I believe that the data strongly support my thesis that income inequality tends to be more than offset by upward income mobility over time. The same can be said of the distribution of wealth.

Live Long and Prosper

Progressives rarely consider the possibility that demographic trends might significantly exaggerate income and wealth inequality. For example, they never adjust their favorite measure of median household income to reflect the decline in the average size of households since the early 1960s (Fig. 79). They don't mention that the percentage of the civilian, noninstitutional working-age population (16 years and older) that has never been married has been rising for years (Fig. 80). It is up from 22.1% at the start of the data during June 1976 to 32.5% during June 2021. A persistent and significant increase in the number of households with singles and unmarried couples could certainly be an underlying cause of rising inequality.

The age structure of US households undoubtedly has had a significant impact on income distribution. (See Appendix Table 8.) From 2001 to 2019, the number of households rose 20.4 million led by an 18.6 million increase in the number of them with the head of the household 55 years old or older. The aging of the Baby Boom generation accounted for this development. Indeed, the oldest of them turned 55 during 2001 and 75 during 2021.

The Census data series on mean household incomes tend to rise as the heads of the households age. Incomes tend to peak when the heads are 45 to 54 years old. Then household incomes tend to decline in the 10 years before and after the head passes the traditional retirement age of 65. (See Appendix Table 8.) The huge generation of Baby Boomers naturally has impacted income inequality given this pattern of rising incomes among older households. Many Boomers have been living longer than past generations and have been working longer beyond the traditional retirement age. As they retire, the mean incomes of younger households should get a boost.

Demographic trends can also skew wealth inequality studies. It should come as no surprise that the share of net worth of households held by the Baby Boom generation has increased from 21.3% during the third quarter of 1989 to 52.2% during the first quarter of 2021 (Fig. 81). Over this period, their net worth has increased 1,436% from $4.4 trillion to $67.6 trillion (Fig. 82).

As the Baby Boomers get older and pass away, many of their GenX, Millennials, and Gen Z descendants stand to benefit from large inheritances. In any event, as these younger generations age, their incomes and wealth will increase as long as progressives don't make too much more progress with their progressive agenda.

My discussion of income and wealth inequality and mobility is consistent with the "Schumpeter Hotel." Economist Joseph Schumpeter (mentioned in Chapter 1) likened income distribution to the rooms in a hotel. The best rooms are on the top floor, but there are few of them. Those on the middle floors are standard and more plentiful. There are lots of substandard rooms in the lower floors. On any given night, the hotel's guests experience very unequal accommodations. Later, though, the same people either remain on their floor or move to better or worse floors. My analysis of the data suggests that in America's competitive economy the hotel continues to be refurbished, providing better rooms to more people.

Finally, I should note that there have been various studies of the Forbes 400 list of the wealthiest Americans by total estimated net worth, regardless of their income during any given year. Since the list was started in 1982, there has been lots of turnover, as some members experienced reversals of fortune (or passed away) and as people who weren't even born back then are now on the list. The top 400 today are certainly much wealthier than the top 400 in 1982, but they aren't the same people!

Most of the Forbes 400 tend to be older Americans. Income and wealth inequality may be less about rich versus poor than old versus young. As *Star Trek*'s Mr. Spock once said: "Live long and prosper."

Chapter 8
Profitable and Unprofitable Policies

Stake in the Heart

It is widely recognized that progressives have been winning the culture wars in our universities and media for quite some time. Now they are aiming to force corporations to take their side in their epic battle against capitalism. They have already made a great deal of progress on this front. "Profits" isn't a four-letter word, but progressives have managed to make it so as more and more business executives prefer not to even mention it in their public statements about their goals for their companies.

As I observed in the Introduction, progressives have been pushing corporate managements and boards of directors to respond to the demands of their stakeholders, not just their shareholders. Stakeholders are much needier than shareholders. Meeting stakeholders' long list of needs requires corporations to be managed for the benefit of a multitude of special-interest groups that hold no interest in the company's profitability, being neither investors, customers, employees, or suppliers! Meeting the needs of shareholders simply means growing profits by satisfying customers and attracting more of them.

The central premise of many progressives' stance is that corporations are getting away with something. Those that are primarily managed for profit growth instead of according to progressive principles of social wellbeing must be exploiting someone, the thinking goes. Or at least they must be taking unfair advantage of the economic system. Their profits must come at the expense of someone, whether underpaid workers, over-charged customers, or polluted local communities or society at large. Furthermore, progressives charge that companies don't pay taxes commensurate with their use of public infrastructure.

During the 2012 election campaign, in a speech delivered on July 13 in Roanoke, Virginia, President Barack Obama stated, "Somebody helped to create this unbelievable American system that we have that allowed you to thrive. Somebody invested in roads and bridges. If you've got a business, you didn't build that."[51] Obama's critics protested that he was attacking private property and entrepreneurial capitalism. Obama's campaign responded that he only meant that roads and bridges are built by the government, not by business.

A more blunt expression of this progressive notion was pre-viously provided by Senator Warren, who won her Senate seat in 2012. In an August 2011 campaign speech, she defended pro-gressive economic policies. In a viral video of her talk before an audience in Andover, Massachusetts, she famously said:[52]

> I hear all this, you know, 'Well, this is class warfare, this is whatever.' No. There is nobody in this country who got rich on his own—nobody. You built a factory out there? Good for you. But I want to be clear. You moved your goods to mar-ket on the roads the rest of us paid for. You hired workers the rest of us paid to educate. You were safe in your factory because of police-forces and fire-forces that the rest of us paid for. You didn't have to worry that marauding bands would come and seize everything at your factory—and hire someone to protect against this—because of the work the rest of us did. Now look, you built a factory and it turned into something terrific, or a great idea. God bless—keep a big hunk of it. But part of the underlying social contract is,

you take a hunk of that and pay forward for the next kid who comes along.

On August 19, 2019, the Business Roundtable (BRT), a group consisting of 181 CEOs of America's largest corporations issued a remarkable statement titled "Business Roundtable Redefines the Purpose of a Corporation to Promote 'An Economy That Serves All Americans.'" It endorsed the progressive notion that companies should be managed for the benefit of stakeholders rather than shareholders. Jamie Dimon, Chairman and CEO of JPMorgan Chase & Co. and the BRT's chairman, said, "The American dream is alive, but fraying. Major employers are investing in their workers and communities because they know it is the only way to be successful over the long term. These modernized principles reflect the business community's unwavering commitment to continue to push for an economy that serves all Americans."[53]

Almost in passing, the statement endorsed "the free-market system" as "the best means of generating good jobs, a strong and sustainable economy, innovation, a healthy environment and economic opportunity for all." The statement then defined "the purpose of a corporation" as fulfilling several commitments to six stakeholders, including customers ("meeting or exceeding customer expectations"), employees ("compensating them fairly" and "supporting them" to "develop new skills" and fostering "diversity and inclusion"), suppliers ("serving as good partners" so they can "help meet our mission"), and communities (protecting the environment "by embracing sustainable practices").

Remarkably, last, and by implication least, is the corporation's commitment to its owners, the shareholders. The word "profit" isn't mentioned once. The only commitment to shareholders is "transparency and effective engagement."

By the way, a growing number of business schools are asking their graduates to recite the MBA Oath.[54] It is consistent with the ideology of the BRT statement, pledging to do right by society. The oath keepers promise to be ethical and to protect human rights and the planet. The goal is to "create sustainable and inclusive prosperity." Not mentioned even once is the word "profits."

The new BRT statement was immediately criticized by the Council of Institutional Investors (CII). In an August 19, 2019 response, the CII stated:

> The BRT statement suggests corporate obligations to a variety of stakeholders, placing shareholders last, and referencing shareholders simply as providers of capital rather than as owners. CII believes boards and managers need to sustain a focus on long-term shareholder value. To achieve long-term shareholder value, it is critical to respect stakeholders, but also to have clear accountability to company owners.[55]

The CII critique noted, "Accountability to everyone means accountability to no one." It also observed that the BRT statement "seems to downplay or ignore the role of markets." Managing a company for stakeholders rather than for shareholders could drive up the costs of doing business and depress profits. Granted, there are more and more shareholders who value companies with good Environmental, Social, and Governance (ESG) scores. They are unlikely to do so for very long if those companies fail to deliver profits growth. Unprofitable companies that check all the boxes for their stakeholders but not their shareholders aren't likely to expand their payrolls and capacity. Unprofitable companies worsen rather than improve general prosperity.

The Wall Street Journal's editorial board also critiqued the BRT statement on August 19, 2019.[56] The editorial bemoaned the fact that "the CEOs for America's biggest companies feel the need to distance themselves from their owners." It noted that the 300-word BRT statement doesn't get around to mentioning "shareholders" until the second-to-last paragraph. The statement instead stressed "a fundamental commitment to all of our stakeholders."

The editorial detected "more than a whiff of preemptive politics." The CEOs know that socialism is on the rise in America, making them prime political targets for progressive politicians. The CEOs' lame attempt to convince these politicians that they are on their side may simply provide the progressives with the political rope to hang the CEOs, according to the editorial.

The editorial noted that the big advantage of the shareholder model is that "it focuses the corporate mission on measurable financial results." Profits are easy to measure. ESG scores are very subjective, and their impact on profits is more likely to be negative than positive. The editorial warned, "An ill-defined stakeholder model can quickly become a license for CEOs to waste capital on projects that might make them local or political heroes but ill-serve those same stakeholders if the business falters."

The intellectual Godfather of the shareholder model was Milton Friedman. In a September 13, 1970 op-ed in the *New York Times Magazine*, he discussed what would come to be known as "the Friedman Doctrine," or the "shareholder theory of capitalism."[57] From the start, he pulled no punches, characterizing proponents of the "social responsibility of business" as "preaching pure and simple socialism." He denied that corporations have responsibilities. "Only people can have responsibilities," he wrote.

Friedman observed that "in a free-enterprise, private-property system, a corporate executive is an employee of the owners of the business. He has direct responsibility to his employers. That responsibility is to conduct the business in accordance with their desires, which generally will be to make as much money as possible while conforming to the basic rules of the society, both those embodied in law and those embodied in ethical custom."

The corporate executive is the agent of the shareholders, i.e., the owners of the firm. If he is acting in ways that are not in the best interest of his employers, then his actions come at their expense. He is spending their money when he bases his business decisions on what he deems to be good for society rather than on what benefits his shareholders.

It's up to Congress to enact laws that require corporations to behave in ways that benefit society. It's up to corporate executives to maximize profits within the context and spirit of the laws of the land. Social responsibilities should be determined by the political process, not by corporate managers, who "can do good—but only at their own expense."

Friedman provided a warning in 1970 to the CEOs who signed the BRT statement in 2019. Promoting social responsibility may gain business executives "kudos in the short run. But it helps to strengthen the already too prevalent view that the pursuit of profits is wicked and immoral and must be curbed and controlled by external forces." He concluded that in a free society "there is one and only one social responsibility of business— to use its resources and engage in activities designed to increase its profits so long as it stays within the rules of the game, which is to say, engages in open and free competition without deception or fraud."

Updating Friedman's warning, Stephen Soukup provided an outstanding wake-up call about the politicization of America's business and capital markets in his 2021 book *The Dictatorship of Woke Capitalism*. He observes that this development is just one of many ongoing assaults by progressives to win the culture wars in America by winning the hearts and minds of the people who run the major institutions of our country. These institutions include the universities, the media, and the government. Progressives have seen many of their policies embraced and implemented by progressive presidents, including Teddy Roosevelt, Woodrow Wilson, Franklin Roosevelt, John Kennedy, Lyndon Johnson, Jimmy Carter, Bill Clinton, Barack Obama, and Joe Biden. They have become increasingly influential in the Democratic Party in recent years.

Soukup observes that, until recently, corporate America managed to stay apolitical and focused on profits. No more. The big break for progressives came with Wall Street's embrace of the ESG movement. More and more investors with environmental, social, and governance agendas require that the companies they own should disclose what they are doing to achieve ESG goals that may have nothing to do with profitability or may even reduce it. In the past, government regulators such as the Securities and Exchange Commission (SEC) required publicly listed companies to disclose information that could have a "material" impact on profits. Now the SEC is moving toward requiring disclosure of ESG-related developments whether or not they have a material impact on profits.

On June 28, Allison Herren Lee, an SEC commissioner and its acting chair, gave the keynote address at the 2021 Society for Corporate Governance National Conference.[58] She observed, "Increasingly, boards of directors are called upon to navigate the challenges presented by climate change, racial injustice, economic inequality, and numerous other issues that are fundamental to the success and sustainability of companies, financial markets, and our economy."

She acknowledged that this is a controversial subject, but clearly sided with stakeholders rather than shareholders. Corporations, she argued, have too much influence over all aspects of our lives to be allowed to focus just on profits. "Small wonder, then, that not just investors, but employees, consumers, vendors, suppliers, and numerous other stakeholders, look to companies to design and implement long-term, sustainable policies that support growth and address the environmental and social impacts these companies have." She noted that the SEC is considering "potential rulemaking to improve climate and other ESG disclosures for investors." She also declared that "[t]hose days are over" for the Milton Friedman era of maximizing value for shareholders. She explicitly supported large institutional investors like BlackRock that are using their clout as shareholders to threaten boards of directors to give more weight to ESG or be held accountable if they fall short.

Harvard Professor George Serafeim is ready, willing, and able to provide ESG scores on corporations to the SEC, BlackRock, and any other interested parties. He was featured in a December 1, 2020 Bloomberg article titled "How Wrong Was Milton Friedman? Harvard Team Quantifies the Ways."[59] The professor claims that profits and losses aren't enough for investors to determine the impact that a company is having on people and the planet. He and his team at Harvard are quantifying ESG factors. "What we're doing is empowering capitalism to really have free and fair markets," Serafeim said. "Otherwise, it's kind of a crony version of it." Ironically, this is all very similar to the Social Credit System that the Chinese Communist Party has imposed on its people to determine who is a good citizen and who is a bad one. The former is rewarded, while the latter is punished, by the government. Similarly, in the US, companies with bad ESG scores risk getting blacklisted by stakeholders and even the government.

A July 13, 2021 Bloomberg Green article raised some serious questions about the ESG agenda that BlackRock has been steamrolling into corporate boardrooms.[60] Asking the questions is someone who should know the answers, namely, Tariq Fancy, the former chief investment officer for sustainable investing at BlackRock. He and "a small but growing cohort of disillusioned veterans are speaking out against efforts by corporations and investors to address an overheating planet, income inequality and other big societal problems," according to the article.

Fancy left BlackRock in 2019. In January 2020, the firm's chief executive officer, Larry Fink, said BlackRock put sustainability at the center of its investments by voting against corporate directors who fail to create plans to transition to a low-carbon economy as required by Fink & Co.[61] In a March 16, 2021 *USA Today* op-ed, Fancy wrote, "In truth, sustainable investing boils down to little more than marketing hype, PR spin and disingenuous promises from the investment community." He charged that ESG is an investment fad marketed by promoters "all in the name of profits."[62] He should know.

This is an excellent example of how the profit motive becomes corrupted in the selfish version of capitalism, i.e., crony capitalism.

Corporations are becoming increasingly politicized. Progressives, who usually decry corporate involvement in politics as a corrupting abuse of free speech, are demanding that firms speak up about social issues. More than a hundred top executives and corporate leaders gathered online in early April 2021 to discuss their response to voting laws under consideration in several states and already enacted in Georgia. They mostly blasted these laws as being too restrictive.

Senate Minority Leader Mitch McConnell (R-KY) warned big businesses that they would face "serious consequences" after accusing them of employing "economic blackmail" in attempts to influence voting laws.[63] "From election law to environmentalism to radical social agendas to the Second Amendment, parts of the private sector keep dabbling in behaving like a woke parallel government," the Kentucky Republican said in an April 5, 2021 statement. "Corporations will invite serious consequences if they become a vehicle for far-left mobs to hijack our country from outside the constitutional order."

It is noteworthy that many of these same American business executives have no trouble doing business in China. They certainly haven't organized any online sessions to object to the totalitarian practices of the Chinese Communist Party, including systematic human rights abuses. Hypocrisy is a quintessential trait of crony capitalism.

Taxation Without Representation

Willie Sutton was a bank robber who lived from 1901 through 1980. During his 40-year robbery career, he stole an estimated $2 million, and he eventually spent more than half of his adult life in prison and escaped three times. He reputedly replied to a reporter's inquiry about why he robbed banks by saying "because that's where the money is." In Sutton's 1976 book *Where the Money Was*, Sutton denies having said this, but added that "If anybody had asked me, I'd have probably said it."

Why are corporations taxed? Ask any politician that question, especially progressive ones, and they are likely to admit, "because that's where the money is." A corporate income tax was first enacted in 1894, but a key aspect of it was shortly held unconstitutional. In 1909, Congress enacted an excise tax on corporations based on income. After ratification of the Sixteenth Amendment to the US Constitution on February 3, 1913, this became the corporate provisions of the federal income tax.

The main argument against taxing corporations is that it results in double taxation. The corporation pays taxes on its profits. The shareholders pay taxes on the dividends that are distributed from after-tax profits by the corporation. Undistributed profits that are reinvested in a corporation could boost the stock price of the firm and be taxed as capital gains of shareholders who sell their stock.

Based on my analysis in this study, a zero corporate tax rate would increase both the dividends paid to shareholders and undistributed profits, boosting corporate cash flow. That would lower the government's corporate tax receipts to zero but would boost tax receipts from the personal income taxes paid on dividends. More corporate cash flow would cause corporations to expand by increasing their payrolls and capital spending. As the number of workers increases along with their wages, so would the individual income tax and payroll tax receipts. A zero corporate tax rate would also allow managements to spend more time on managing their companies to boost their profits than on finding ways to reduce their tax bill.

One might argue: But that can't be right! They should pay their fair share.

It depends on whether the goal is fairness, which is a highly subjective and controversial concept, or prosperity, which is easy to measure. We are likely to get more jobs, more productivity, higher real wages, and even more government revenues if we promote more corporate-led prosperity with a zero corporate tax rate.

Of course, the chances of that happening are slim to none. The current Biden administration in Washington is pushing to raise taxes and regulations on business in all sorts of ways. It's hard to predict what will be the outcome of this effort. In any event, corporate income taxes have tended to contribute around just 10% of US federal government tax receipts. The major sources of revenues have been individual income taxes and payroll taxes (Fig. 83).

In August 2021, Senator Warren proposed a minimum tax on the profits of the nation's richest companies. The measure would require the most profitable companies to pay a 7% tax on the earnings they report to investors—a.k.a. their annual book value—above $100 million. An August 9, 2021 article in *The New York Times* explained, "By taxing the earnings reported to investors, not to the Internal Revenue Service, Democrats would be hitting earnings that companies like to maximize, not the earnings they try hard to diminish for tax purposes."[64] The idea for this "real corporate profits tax" rate was the brainchild of the aforementioned dynamic progressive duo of Saez and Zucman. They estimated that about 1,300 public corporations would be impacted by the policy, generating close to $700 billion between 2023 and 2032.

Capping Cronies

I wholeheartedly agree with progressives who want to reduce corporate cronyism. There is certainly plenty of room for improvement in corporate governance. I have a few ideas on how to do so, including limiting the number of boards on which an individual may serve.

I'm not sure about the best way to cap executive compensation, but it does need to be capped. While the Economic Policy Institute has been wrong on the issue of wage stagnation, this progressive think tank is right about the excessive pay received by CEOs. An August 18, 2020 press release authored by Lawrence Mishel and Jori Kandra of the EPI reported that, in 2019, a CEO at one of the top 350 firms in the US was paid $21.3 million on average. That's 320 times as much as a typical worker earns (Fig. 84). This ratio is up from 293-to-1 in 2018, 61-to-1 in 1989, and 21-to-1 in 1965. The CEOs are even making six times as much as the One Percent! The EPI researchers used a "realized" measure of CEO pay that counts stock awards when vested and stock options when cashed in rather than when granted.[65]

The EPI notes that about three-quarters of CEO pay is stock-related. That's truly ironic. Progressive President Bill Clinton changed the tax code in 1993, when he signed into law his first budget, creating Section 162(m) of the Internal Revenue Code. This provision placed a $1 million limit on the amount that corporations could treat as a tax-deductible expense for compensation paid to the top five executives. It was hoped that would put an end to skyrocketing executive pay.[66]

The law of unintended consequences trumped the new tax provision, which had a huge flaw—it exempted "performance-based" pay, such as stock options, from the $1 million cap. Businesses started paying executives more in stock options, and top executive pay continued to soar. Progressive critics, notably Senator Warren, concluded that the 1993 tax-code change had backfired badly and that soaring executive pay has exacerbated income inequality.

On January 25, 2011, the SEC implemented "Say-on-Pay" requirements in Section 951 of the Dodd-Frank Wall Street Reform and Consumer Protection Act, which President Barack Obama had signed into law in July 2010. Public companies that are subject to proxy voting rules must provide their shareholders with an advisory vote on the compensation of the most highly paid executives. These votes must be held at least once every three years. These companies are required to disclose compensation arrangements and understandings with those executive officers in connection with an acquisition or merger. In certain circumstances, these companies are also required to conduct a shareholder advisory vote to approve the golden parachute compensation arrangements.[67] The outcome of say-on-pay is nonbinding. Boards of directors aren't required to make changes to compensation plans even if a majority of shareholders vote against the proposed pay package.

The problem is that all too often, CEOs are involved in selecting the members of their boards, who are paid as much as $250,000 to $300,000 for a few days of work per year. The CEOs certainly have an incentive to provide these lucrative positions to people they know are likely to be generous when it comes to executive pay. The board members have an incentive not to rock the boat, siding with management on most issues rather than with activist shareholders pushing for changes.

In theory, nonexecutive board members should be 100% independent of management. In practice, cronyism is rampant in corporate America. Two experts on corporate governance at Morningstar, Kristoffer Inton and Joshua Aguilar, have suggested that the "nominating and compensation committee needs to be completely independent and free of the CEO's influence, especially when the CEO is also the chairperson." They also believe that "board members should have equity in the company, but they should be obligated to purchase their stakes, not just get them for free, and at a level that matters to their wealth. This would tie their fates to those of the shareholders they represent."[68]

SEC Commissioner Robert J. Jackson, Jr., who was appointed by President Donald Trump, also had some good ideas on how to regulate some games played by corporate executives with buybacks. In a June 11, 2018 speech, he discussed "how to give corporate managers incentives to create sustainable long-term value."[69] When he joined the SEC in early 2018, he asked his staff to study 385 buybacks over the previous 15 months. Jackson was shocked to learn this: "In *half* of the buybacks we studied, at least one executive sold shares in the month following the buyback announcement. In fact, *twice as many companies* have insiders selling in the eight days after a buyback announcement as sell on an ordinary day. So right after the company tells the market that the stock is cheap, executives overwhelmingly decide to sell."

To fix this problem, Jackson favored adopting an SEC rule that would "encourage executives to keep their skin in the game for the long term." In his opinion, safe harbor from securities-fraud liability should be denied to companies that choose to allow executives to cash out during a buyback.

Another troubling development in corporate governance, as discussed above, is the concentration of stock ownership among a handful of passive investment funds, such as BlackRock. That is giving immense power to BlackRock's management to impose its views on corporate America on behalf of all the investors in its ETFs and mutual funds. The money manager casts a long shadow, voting on behalf of investors in shareholder meetings, sitting on boards of directors, and helping to decide executives' pay packages and other company matters.

BlackRock's management has adopted a very progressive agenda for their company. That's fine. However, what gives BlackRock's management the right to impose their views on other company managements? Oh yes, the firm is a major shareholder of those companies. But in reality, the shareholders are individual and institutional investors who invest in BlackRock's funds. Does BlackRock's management really represent them?

BlackRock's management is very well connected in Washington, DC. This situation smacks of crony capitalism in which Big Business and Big Government decide what's best for all of us.

Progressives are always championing using antitrust laws to break up big business enterprises on the grounds that they have too much market power and reduce competition. It's time to consider whether the concentration of power over corporate governance matters by a handful of passive management firms meets the criteria for antitrust enforcement action.

Meanwhile, perhaps BlackRock can use its power to rein in CEO compensation. The firm can set a good example on corporate governance by starting with its own executives. CEO Fink's total compensation rose to $29.85 million in 2020, an 18.2% increase from $25.25 million in the prior year, according to the company's proxy statement. The largest portion of his 2020 compensation—$14.9 million—was from a long-term incentive award, followed by cash at $9.5 million; deferred equity, $3.95 million; and base salary, $1.5 million. The firm's compensation committee rated Mr. Fink's 2020 performance as "far exceeding" expectations.

JPMorgan's CEO Jamie Dimon, who is also the chair of the BRT, received $31.5 million in compensation during 2020—the same as 2019—mostly in restricted stock he gets if the bank hits certain performance hurdles. During July 2020, the bank's board of directors granted Dimon, who was 65 years old, a retention bonus in the form of 1.5 million options that he can exercise in 2026, according to a regulatory filing. The award, valued at $50 million when issued, required Mr. Dimon to stay at the bank the whole time and hit certain performance targets to receive the full amount.

The Federal Reserve, it turns out, has played a very important role in boosting CEO compensation and exacerbating income and wealth inequality. The Fed was established in 1914 by the administration of progressive President Woodrow Wilson. Under Fed Chairs Janet Yellen and now Jerome Powell, the central bank's policies turned increasingly progressive. Yellen, who was Fed chair from February 2014 through February 2018, monitored a "dashboard" of employment indicators to emphasize that she was giving more weight to labor market issues.

On Thursday, August 27, 2020, at the annual Jackson Hole economic policy symposium sponsored by the Federal Reserve Bank of Kansas City, Powell announced that the Fed had amended its "Statement on Longer-Run Goals and Monetary Policy Strategy."[70] The Fed reiterated its commitment to its statutory mandate from the Congress of promoting maximum employment and stable prices. However, it literally placed a heightened focus on achieving the employment goal by moving the discussion of employment ahead of inflation, i.e., higher up in the statement.[71] In his speech, like a true-blue progressive, Powell emphasized that "maximum employment is a broad-based and inclusive goal."

In response to the pandemic, the Fed lowered the federal funds rate to zero on March 15, 2020 and commenced yet another program of quantitative easing on March 23, entailing large open-ended purchases of bonds. The Fed maintained this policy through the summer of 2021, even though inflation was heating up. Powell declared that this would be a "transitory" development and insisted that monetary policy needed to remain accommodative to achieve the Fed's maximum employment goal.

The consequence of the Fed's ultra-easy monetary policies in response to the pandemic was to send the stock market to record highs. The historically low interest rates resulting from the Fed's progressive monetary policies forced investors to overweight equities relative to bonds, thus pushing stock prices higher. The

S&P 500 doubled on a closing basis from its trough of 2,237.40 on March 23, 2020 through August 16, 2021. It took the market 354 trading days to get there, marking the fastest bull market doubling off a bottom since World War II, according to a CNBC analysis of data from S&P Dow Jones Indices.[72]

That certainly bolstered the incomes of lots of CEOs, such as Fink and Dimon, with pay packages heavily skewed toward stock compensation. Perhaps they are business geniuses and deserve every penny that they are paid. Then again, as Humphrey B. Neill, the father of contrarian investing, famously observed: "Don't confuse brains with a bull market!"

Meanwhile, lots of households that depend on fixed-income returns saw their incomes dive. Wealth inequality was exacerbated too by soaring equity values, though home prices also soared. The widespread appreciation of many asset prices raised concerns that the "bubble in everything" would eventually burst. I have to conclude that the Fed's progressive-leaning policies aimed at maximizing employment have contributed greatly to income and wealth inequality.

Academic Racket

I also agree with progressives on the importance of education in reducing income inequality and in enhancing upward income mobility. However, as progressives have gained more power to set the agenda for our institutions of higher education, the cost of education has risen prohibitively. The CPI for college tuition and fees has increased a staggering 1,435% from January 1978 through July 2021, more than four times faster than the overall CPI's 334% increase.

As a result, student loans have soared, causing many college graduates to start their careers weighed down by these loans.

Data available since the first quarter of 2006 show that student loans have increased by 260% through the second quarter of 2021 to $1.73 trillion.

The academic market needs more competition. Colleges have been getting fat on the higher tuitions they can charge because of the availability of student loans. Ending federal student loan programs might force colleges to be run more like lean, profit-driven businesses and to do a better job for their customers.

It is widely recognized that there is a strong correlation between getting a good education and income mobility. Many studies have also shown that there is plenty of room for improvement when it comes to providing a good education to students from low-income households. This has been a vexing problem that progressives have attempted to solve for quite some time with various policy initiatives.

The profit motive may very well provide a market-driven path to open up more and better educational opportunities for more people. In Chapter 6, I examined recent widespread labor shortages and concluded that they are not solely due to the pandemic. They are more structural in nature because they are attributable to demographic trends. Many businesses are likely to respond to this challenge by doing all they can to boost the productivity of their available workers.

Companies are offering their employees more opportunities for career advancement through training programs to improve their skills. Some companies are providing tuition assistance as an incentive to improve recruitment and retention of workers. Free or discounted higher education cuts down on student debt while enhancing the long-term wellbeing of employees. They are likely to reciprocate with greater loyalty to their employer.

Education as an employee benefit has been around for a while; some companies long have paid for business-school programs to help their white-collar workers advance. What's different now is that companies are extending this benefit to more of their employees and promoting it more than ever before. Employer-sponsored education is a win-win concept for all concerned. So is profit-driven prosperity.

Stocks as a Birth Right

Finally, I have a simple idea for increasing Americans' appreciation of the importance of corporate profits. The federal government likes to give money away. Why not establish an automatic $1,000 savings account for all babies born in 2022 and beyond? That would cost a bit less than $4 billion per year if live births rebound back to the pre-pandemic annual pace of about 3.7 million. The funds would be invested in an S&P 500 exchange-traded fund. Dividends would be automatically reinvested. Beneficiaries would be allowed to have access to the proceeds on a tax-free basis once they turn 65 years old.

Since the end of 1935, the S&P 500 total return index has been rising around 10% per year (Fig. 85). Applying this growth rate to a single $1,000 investment starting next year and compounded annually would provide each beneficiary in 2087 with $600,000 in current dollars. That would teach Americans born from 2022 onward the power of profits and compounding dividends on a tax-free basis. Capitalism's fans would grow along with their "Birth Right Portfolios."

Epilogue

Confessions of an Entrepreneurial Capitalist

I am an entrepreneurial capitalist. Yardeni Research is an S corporation. I employ 10 people (eight full-time and two part-time) and four independent contractors. We operate as a team.

After many years on Wall Street, I opened my own firm at the start of 2007. It was an exhilarating and challenging experience. For the first time in my career, I had to meet a payroll. Doing so was a huge responsibility to my employees and their families. If the business didn't work out, not only would I be out of a job, but so would all my employees.

I must say that I've never worked harder or enjoyed working more than after I went out on my own. Running my own company has been a great learning experience about entrepreneurial capitalism. As a small business owner, I've come to understand first hand why entrepreneurs are driven by insecurity, not selfishness. My number-one worry is that if my team doesn't satisfy our customers' needs, our customers will go elsewhere, putting us out of business. That's why we strive so hard to grow our business. Growth confirms that we are doing right by our customers in the competitive market. This requires that we put our customers first, not ourselves.

A key goal of our business model is to go viral: "If you like our products and services, tell your friends." There always are opportunities to gain customers by outperforming our competitors. Milton Friedman observed that when customers are free to choose among competing producers, consumers always win. The producers only win if they satisfy their customers. If they do so, that will be reflected in their profits.

It follows that the most profitable companies aren't the ones run by the greediest people. Rather, they are the ones that cater best to the needs of consumers. Of course, profits can always be boosted temporarily by shortchanging workers and cutting corners on quality. However, in competitive markets, your best workers can always find jobs with competitors who are profitable because they are winning the hearts, minds, and budgets of consumers. And your customers can find those competitors in a heartbeat, if dissatisfied. Companies with the happiest customers are also likely to have the happiest employees.

Admittedly, this is an idealized version of entrepreneurial capitalism, which does exist in the United States in many industries, especially the ones with lots of pass-through businesses, which I discussed in Chapter 4. However, it also coexists with crony capitalism.

I have no trade association, lobbyists, or political cronies in Washington, DC to protect my interests. So the forces of the competitive market compel me to work as hard as possible to satisfy my customers more than my competitors do. Happily, when I visit our accounts, they tell me that we are one of the select economic and investment research firms on which they rely. However, they tend to have relatively fixed budgets, so they always have the option of dropping our research and signing up with one of our competitors. If their budgets get cut, all we can do is hope that they decide to keep us and drop someone else.

The bottom line is that in a competitive market, the pressure is on to be better than your best competitor. My market is full of top-notch competitors. That's great for our customers, who can choose whichever of us provides them with the best service at the right price. My firm has been in business for 14 years now, so we've done well. I must thank our competitors for keeping us at the top of our game and our accounts for choosing our investment research service.

The above might seem a bit like a commercial for my firm. Well, I am an entrepreneurial capitalist, after all.

Conserving Progress

In the movie *Doctor Zhivago* (1965), Dr. Yuri Zhivago returns home after World War I to find that his spacious house in Moscow has been divided into tenements by the local Communist government. As he and his wife are walking upstairs to their assigned quarters, Comrade Kaprugina, the chairman of the residence committee, scolds him in front of his new cohabitants, saying, "There was living space for 13 families in this one house!" A disoriented Zhivago sheepishly responds, "Yes, yes, this is a better arrangement, Comrades. More just."[73]

Communists have a long history of reducing income inequality by getting rid of the rich and making nearly everyone equally poor. They eliminate wealth inequality simply by confiscating and banning private property. That's how they solve the fairness question, by imposing "more just" arrangements.

Most progressives aren't that extreme, but they regularly call on the government to increase taxes on the wealthy and on businesses to redistribute their "unfair" gains. They have an all too simplistic view of our economy that is based on the hackneyed class warfare model, which has become less and less relevant over the past 70 years or so. In some ways, they can take credit for improving the lot of the working class, thus easing their conflict with the capitalist class. However, progressives are never satisfied with their successes and always find fault in the economic system that they've significantly helped to create.

Again, there's no question that income and wealth inequalities are a consequence of capitalism, but so is upward income mobility. That's especially true during periods of prosperity. Most importantly, though, is the reality that prosperity is the greatest consequence of capitalism.

Economic inequality will always exist in a competitive economy driven by the profit motive. However, such inequality hasn't gotten much worse in recent decades, as progressives incessantly claim; their claims fly in the face of lots of contradictory evidence, such as the solid gains in the standards of living of most Americans as measured by inflation-adjusted average personal consumption per household.

I challenge progressives who claim income inequality has worsened to prove that this is so after taxes and after government support payments have been considered, not before. If they're still right, then their calls for more income redistribution are more justified. However, before pressing for even more income redistribution, they should also prove that the existing redistribution programs are not the cause of worsening pretax and pre-benefits income inequality. Conservatives argue that government benefits erode the work ethic and thereby exacerbate income inequality. I generally agree with that view. The debate rages on.

In my view, which I've supported with lots of data in this study, the capitalist juices are still flowing strongly in the United States. Profits are growing and driving productivity and prosperity. In America, the consuming class is the only class that really matters. We are all consumers, and we are all beneficiaries of the competitive pressures driving producers and their employees to offer us goods and services at the lowest possible prices and with the best quality.

Entrepreneurial capitalism is flourishing in the United States, as evidenced by the rapid growth in sole proprietorships and other pass-through business enterprises. As a result, standards of living continue to improve in the United States. Notwithstanding the naysayers, most Americans have never been better off than they are today thanks to record profits and record productivity, which are fueling widespread prosperity.

And this has happened in the face of a pandemic! In fact, we can thank the profit motive and technological innovations for accelerating the pace at which vaccines were developed.

I am an entrepreneurial capitalist. I am also a conservative who champions progress. Let's conserve the system of entrepreneurial capitalism that provides all Americans with the best opportunity to continue to progress.

Appendix

Appendix Table 1:
Number of Tax Returns by Business Entities (million)

	Corporations			Sole Proprietorships	Partnerships (& Partners)	Total Pass-Throughs*
	Total	C	S			
2020	6.8	1.8	5.0	na	na	na
2019	7.3	2.1	5.2	na	na	na
2018	7.2	2.1	5.1	27.1	4.0 (27.4)	36.2
2017	6.3	1.6	4.7	26.4	3.9 (27.5)	35.0
2016	6.2	1.6	4.6	25.5	3.7 (28.2)	33.8
2015	6.1	1.6	4.5	25.2	3.7 (27.1)	33.4
2014	6.0	1.6	4.4	24.6	3.6 (27.7)	32.6
2013	5.9	1.6	4.3	24.1	3.5 (27.5)	31.9
2012	5.8	1.6	4.2	23.6	3.4 (25.3)	31.2
2011	5.8	1.6	4.2	23.4	3.3 (24.4)	30.9
2010	5.8	1.7	4.1	23.0	3.2 (22.4)	30.3
2009	5.8	1.7	4.1	22.7	3.2 (21.1)	30.0
2008	5.8	1.8	4.0	22.6	3.1 (19.3)	29.7
2007	5.9	1.9	4.0	23.1	3.1 (18.5)	30.2
2006	5.9	2.0	3.9	22.0	2.9 (16.7)	28.8
2005	5.7	2.0	3.7	21.4	2.8 (16.2)	27.9
2004	5.5	2.0	3.5	20.6	2.5 (15.6)	26.6
2003	5.3	2.0	3.3	19.7	2.4 (14.1)	25.4
2002	5.3	2.1	3.2	18.9	2.2 (14.3)	24.3
2001	5.1	2.1	3.0	18.3	2.1 (14.2)	23.4
2000	5.0	2.1	2.9	17.9	2.1 (13.7)	22.9
1999	4.9	2.2	2.7	17.6	1.9 (15.9)	22.2
1998	4.8	2.2	2.6	17.4	1.9 (15.7)	21.9
1997	4.7	2.2	2.5	17.2	1.8 (16.2)	21.5

* Sum of S corporations, sole proprietorships, and partnerships. The latter two categories include limited liability companies (LLCs).

Source: Internal Revenue Service, https://www.irs.gov/pub/irs-soi/15otidb1.xls.

IN PRAISE OF PROFITS!

Appendix Table 2: Profits Before Tax* (billion dollars)

	All Corporations	C Corporations	S Corporations	S as % of Total
2012	1,997.4	1,453.0	544.4	27.2
2013	2,010.7	1,457.4	553.3	27.5
2014	2,120.2	1,508.8	611.4	28.8
2015	2,060.5	1,368.8	691.7	33.6
2016	2,023.7	1,324.0	699.7	34.6
2017	2,114.5	1,367.5	747.0	35.3

* Including IVA and CCAdj.
Source: Bureau of Economic Analysis, National Income and Product Accounts.

Appendix Table 3: Dividends (billion dollars)

	All Corporations	C Corporations	S Corporations*	S as % of Total
2012	948.7	571.0	377.7	39.8
2013	1,009.0	640.5	368.5	36.5
2014	1,096.1	687.1	409.0	37.3
2015	1,164.9	693.9	471.0	40.4
2016	1,189.4	719.5	469.9	39.5
2017	1,270.4	757.2	513.2	40.4

* Internal Revenue Service data.
Source: Bureau of Economic Analysis, National Income and Product Accounts.

Appendix Table 4: Dividend Payout Ratios (percent)

	S&P 500 Corporations Using After-Tax Reported Aggregate Earnings	S Corporations Using Pre-Tax Profits
2012	36.1	69.3
2013	34.9	66.6
2014	38.6	66.9
2015	50.1	68.1
2016	48.3	67.2
2017	44.5	68.7

Source: Bureau of Economic Analysis, National Income and Product Accounts.

Appendix Table 5:
US Federal Individual Income Tax Returns and
Adjusted Gross Income by Income Groups

	AGI Group	Individual Returns (millions)			
		2001	2018	Change	% Change
1	All	130.26	153.77	23.51	18.0
2	$0-$50K	92.76	88.93	-3.83	-4.1
3	$50K-$100K	26.46	35.15	8.69	32.8
4	$100K-$200K	8.47	21.15	12.68	149.7
5	$200K-$500K	2.02	6.91	4.89	242.1
6	$500K+	0.55	1.65	1.10	200.0
		Adjusted Gross Income (trillion dollars)			
7	All	6.17	11.64	5.47	88.7
8	$0-$50K	1.82	1.76	-0.06	-3.3
9	$50K-$100K	1.84	2.51	0.67	36.4
10	$100K-$200K	1.11	2.88	1.77	159.5
11	$200K-$500K	0.58	1.97	1.39	239.7
12	$500K+	0.82	2.53	1.71	208.5
		Adjusted Gross Income / Return (thousand dollars)			
13	All	47.4	75.7	28.3	59.7
14	$0-$50K	19.6	19.8	0.2	1.0
15	$50K-$100K	69.5	71.3	1.8	2.6
16	$100K-$200K	131.6	136.1	4.5	3.4
17	$200K-$500K	286.7	285.5	-1.2	-0.4
18	$500K+	1,490.9	1,533.3	42.4	2.8
		Group Returns (percent of total returns)			
19	$0-$50K	71.2	57.8	-13.4	—
20	$50K-$100K	20.3	22.9	2.6	—
21	$100K-$200K	6.5	13.8	7.3	—
22	$200K-$500K	1.6	4.4	2.8	—
23	$500K+	0.4	1.1	0.7	—

Source: Internal Revenue Service.

Appendix Table 6:
US Federal Individual Income Tax
Distribution by Income Groups

AGI Group	Individual Returns (percent of total returns) 2001	2018	Change	Adjusted Gross Income (trillion dollars) 2001	2018	Change
All	100.0	100.0	0.0	6.17	11.64	5.47
$0-$50K	71.2	57.8	-13.4	1.82	1.76	-0.06
$50K-$100K	20.3	22.9	2.6	1.84	2.51	0.67
$100K-$200K	6.5	13.8	7.3	1.11	2.88	1.77
$200K-$500K	1.5	4.5	3.0	0.58	1.97	1.39
$500K+	0.4	1.1	0.7	0.82	2.53	1.71

	Adjusted Gross Income (percent of total AGI) 2001	2018	Change	Taxes Paid (billion dollars) 2001	2018	% Change
All	100.0	100.0	0.0	890	1,540	73.0
$0-$50K	29.5	15.1	-14.4	123	65	-47.2
$50K-$100K	29.8	21.5	-8.3	213	187	-12.2
$100K-$200K	18.1	24.7	6.6	185	321	73.5
$200K-$500K	9.4	16.9	7.5	135	328	143.0
$500K+	13.3	21.7	8.4	232	639	175.4

	Taxes Paid (percent of total taxes) 2001	2018	Change	Taxes Paid (percent of groups' AGI) 2001	2018	Change
All	100.0	100.0	0.0	—	—	—
$0-$50K	13.9	4.2	-9.7	6.8	3.7	-3.1
$50K-$100K	24.0	12.1	-11.9	11.6	7.5	-4.1
$100K-$200K	20.9	20.8	-0.1	16.6	11.1	-5.5
$200K-$500K	15.2	21.3	6.1	23.3	16.6	-6.7
$500K+	26.1	41.5	15.4	28.3	25.3	-3.0

Source: Internal Revenue Service.

Appendix Table 7:
Distribution of Household Net Worth

Item by Household Groups	Levels (trillion dollars)			Shares (percent)		
	Q3-1989	Q1-2021	% Change	Q3-1989	Q1-2021	Change
Net Worth	**20.5**	**129.5**	**531.7**	**100.0**	**100.0**	—
Top 1%	4.8	41.5	764.6	23.4	32.1	8.7
90-99%	7.6	48.8	542.1	37.4	37.7	0.3
50-90%	7.3	36.5	400.0	35.5	28.2	-7.3
Bottom 50%	0.8	2.6	225.0	3.7	2.0	-1.7
Assets	**23.5**	**145.7**	**520.0**	**100.0**	**100.0**	—
Top 1%	4.9	42.3	763.3	20.8	29.0	8.2
90-99%	8.1	52.1	543.2	34.6	35.8	1.2
50-90%	8.8	43.6	395.5	37.5	29.9	-7.6
Bottom 50%	1.7	7.7	352.9	7.2	5.3	-1.9
Liabilities	**3.1**	**16.3**	**425.8**	**100.0**	**100.0**	—
Top 1%	0.1	0.8	700.0	4.0	4.7	0.7
90-99%	0.5	3.3	560.0	16.1	20.5	4.4
50-90%	1.6	7.1	343.8	50.3	43.5	-6.8
Bottom 50%	0.9	5.1	466.7	29.7	31.3	1.6
Corporate Equities*	**2.0**	**37.4**	**1,770.0**	**100.0**	**100.0**	—
Top 1%	0.9	20.0	2,122.2	42.3	53.5	11.2
90-99%	0.8	13.2	1,550.0	39.8	35.2	-4.6
50-90%	0.3	4.0	1,233.3	16.9	10.8	-6.1
Bottom 50%	0.02	0.2	900.0	1.0	0.6	-0.4
Real Estate	**6.9**	**33.8**	**389.9**	**100.0**	**100.0**	—
Top 1%	0.6	4.9	716.7	8.6	14.7	6.1
90-99%	2.1	10.2	385.7	30.1	30.1	0
50-90%	3.4	14.8	335.3	49.6	43.8	-5.8
Bottom 50%	0.8	3.9	387.5	11.8	11.5	-0.3

* Corporate equities and mutual funds.

(Continued)

Appendix Table 7 (cont.):
Distribution of Household Net Worth

Item by Household Groups	Levels (trillion dollars)			Shares (percent)		
	Q3-1989	Q1-2021	% Change	Q3-1989	Q1-2021	Change
Pension Entitlements	**4.5**	**29.9**	**564.4**	**100.0**	**100.0**	—
Top 1%	0.4	1.5	275.0	8.8	5.0	-3.8
90-99%	1.8	14.6	711.1	40.8	48.8	8.0
50-90%	2.1	12.9	514.3	46.2	43.2	-3.0
Bottom 50%	0.2	0.9	350.0	4.3	3.0	-1.3
Noncorporate Equity	**2.9**	**13.1**	**351.7**	**100.0**	**100.0**	—
Top 1%	1.3	7.2	453.8	44.6	54.9	10.3
90-99%	1.0	3.9	290.0	34.9	30.0	-4.9
50-90%	0.6	1.8	200.0	19.0	13.7	-5.3
Bottom 50%	0.04	0.2	400.0	1.5	1.3	-0.2
Debt Securities	**1.2**	**4.2**	**283.1**	**100.0**	**100.0**	—
Top 1%	0.6	1.7	258.3	49.3	40.8	-8.5
90-99%	0.4	1.6	316.7	36.5	38.0	0.5
50-90%	0.2	0.9	350.0	13.0	20.6	6.3
Bottom 50%	.01	0.0	(-100.0)	1.2	0.7	-0.5
Life Insurance	**0.8**	**1.8**	**355.4**	**100.0**	**100.0**	—
Top 1%	0.5	0.6	375.0	13.3	30.7	17.4
90-99%	0.1	0.5	333.3	30.1	28.6	-1.5
50-90%	0.2	0.6	300.0	44.9	33.6	-11.3
Bottom 50%	.04	0.1	150.0	11.7	7.1	-4.6

Source: Federal Reserve Board Financial Accounts of the United States, Distributional Financial Accounts (DFA).

Appendix Table 8:
US Household Income by Age of Householder

Number of Households (millions)			
	2001	2019	% Change
All	108.2	128.6	18.9
15-24	6.4	6.2	-3.1
25-34	19.0	20.6	8.4
35-44	24.1	21.4	-11.2
45-54	22.0	22.1	0.5
55-64	14.3	21.2	48.3
65+	22.5	34.2	52.0
Mean Household Income (thousand dollars)			
	2001	2019	% Change
All	58,208	98,088	68.5
15-24	36,148	59,979	65.9
25-34	55,414	88,931	60.5
35-44	69,088	115,938	67.8
45-54	74,722	125,803	68.4
55-64	63,523	109,321	72.1
65+	23,118	47,357	104.8
Aggregate Household Income (trillion dollars)			
	2001	2019	% Change
All	6.3	12.6	100.0
15-24	0.2	0.4	100.0
25-34	1.1	1.8	63.6
35-44	1.7	2.5	47.1
45-54	1.6	2.8	75.0
55-64	0.9	2.3	155.6
65+	0.5	1.6	220.0
Aggregate Household Income (percent of total)			
	2001	2019	Change
15-24	3.2	3.2	0.0
25-34	17.5	14.3	-3.2
35-44	27.0	19.8	-7.4
45-54	25.4	22.2	-3.2
55-64	14.3	18.3	4.0
65+	7.9	12.7	4.8

Note: All income series are in current dollars.
Source: Census Bureau.

Acknowledgments

My colleagues at Yardeni Research deserve a great deal of credit for helping me to put this study together. Debbie Johnson and Mali Quintana spent countless hours checking the data that are shown in the book's text and charts. Melissa Tagg provided insightful research and fact-checking assistance. Jackie Doherty provided numerous good editorial suggestions. Mary Fanslau helped to administer the project. Geoff Moore and Steve Rybka delivered great tech support.

Our in-house editor, Sandy Cohan, cheerfully and masterfully pulled double duty by editing the book and our daily commentary. Her dedication to making the book happen was impressive.

Tom Clemmons also provided great editorial support. David Wogahn skillfully coordinated the production of the book.

Several professional friends also reviewed the manuscript and provided helpful guidance. They are James Baker, Vineer Bhansali, Andrew Bell, Chuck Davidson, Lacy Hunt, Dec Mullarkey, Simon Owen-Williams, Francis Scotland, Gary Smith, Steve Smith, Jim Solloway, and Douglas Tengdin.

Collectively, they provided many improvements; I take full responsibility for any remaining errors and omissions.

Acronyms and Abbreviations

AGI .... adjusted gross income
AHE .... average hourly earnings
BEA .... Bureau of Economic Analysis
BLS .... Bureau of Labor Statistics
BRT .... Business Round Table
CAGR .... compound annual growth rate
CCA .... capital consumption allowance
CCAdj .... capital consumption adjustment
CFC .... consumption of fixed capital
CII .... Council of Institutional Investors
CPI .... Consumer Price Index
CPI-U .... Consumer Price Index for All Urban Consumers
CPI-U-RS .... Consumer Price Index for all Urban
                       Consumers Research Series
CRM .... customer relationship management
D .... Democrat
DFA .... Distributional Financial Accounts
ECI .... Employment Cost Index
EPI .... Economic Policy Institute
ESG .... environmental, social, and governance
ETF .... exchange-traded fund
EPI .... Economic Policy Institute
ESOP .... Employee Stock Ownership Plan
FASB .... Financial Accounting Standards Board
GAAP .... generally accepted accounting principles
GDP .... gross domestic product
GNP .... gross national product
GSS .... General Social Survey

GVC .... Great Virus Crisis
IBES .... Institutional Brokers Estimate System
IRS .... Internal Revenue Service
IVA .... inventory valuation adjustment
LLC .... limited liability company
NBER .... National Bureau of Economic Research
NFB .... nonfarm business
NFIB .... National Federation of Independent Business
NIPA .... National Income and Product Accounts
NSA .... not seasonally adjusted
PBT .... profits before taxes
PCE .... personal consumption expenditures
PCED .... personal consumption expenditures deflator
R .... Republican
RHC .... real hourly compensation
S&P .... Standard & Poor's
SA .... seasonally adjusted
SAAR .... seasonally adjusted annual rate
SEC .... Securities and Exchange Commission
SOI .... statistics of income
ULC .... unit labor costs
YRI .... Yardeni Research, Inc.

Author's Note

This study is another in a series of Topical Studies examining issues that I discussed in my book *Predicting the Markets: A Professional Autobiography* (2018), but in greater detail and on a more current basis. Previous studies in this series, which are available on my Amazon Author Page, include:

The Fed and the Great Virus Crisis (2021)

S&P 500 Earnings, Valuation, and the Pandemic (2020)

Fed Watching for Fun and Profit (2020)

Stock Buybacks: The True Story (2019)

The Yield Curve: What Is It Really Predicting? (2019)

The charts at the end of this study were current as of August 2021. They are available in color along with linked endnotes at **www.yardenibook.com/studies**.

Institutional investors are invited to sign up for the Yardeni Research service on a complimentary trial basis at **yardeni.com/trial**.

Figures

Figure 1.

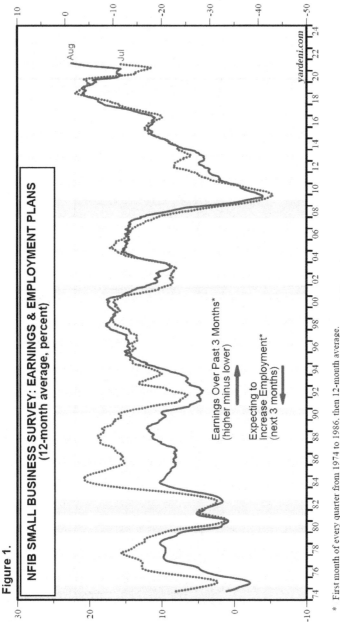

NFIB SMALL BUSINESS SURVEY: EARNINGS & EMPLOYMENT PLANS
(12-month average, percent)

Earnings Over Past 3 Months*
(higher minus lower)

Expecting to
Increase Employment*
(next 3 months)

yardeni.com

* First month of every quarter from 1974 to 1986, then 12-month average.
Note: Shaded areas are recessions according to the National Bureau of Economic Research.
Source: National Federation of Independent Business.

Figure 2.

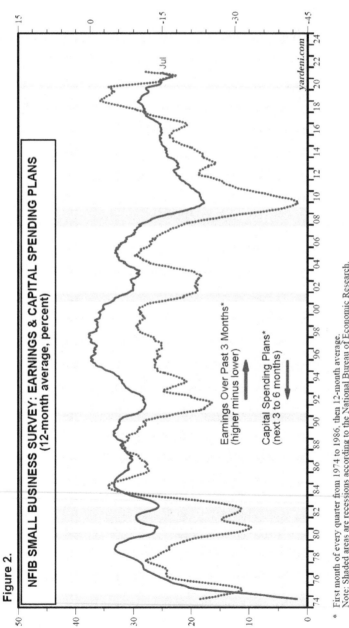

NFIB SMALL BUSINESS SURVEY: EARNINGS & CAPITAL SPENDING PLANS
(12-month average, percent)

Earnings Over Past 3 Months*
(higher minus lower)

Capital Spending Plans*
(next 3 to 6 months)

* First month of every quarter from 1974 to 1986, then 12-month average.
Note: Shaded areas are recessions according to the National Bureau of Economic Research.
Source: National Federation of Independent Business.

Figure 3.

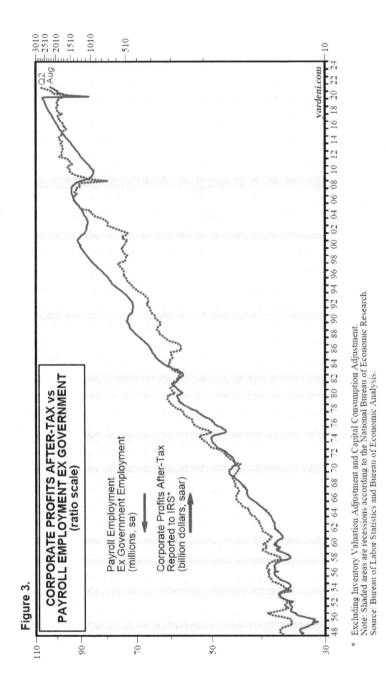

CORPORATE PROFITS AFTER-TAX vs PAYROLL EMPLOYMENT EX GOVERNMENT
(ratio scale)

Payroll Employment
Ex Government Employment
(millions, sa)

Corporate Profits After-Tax
Reported to IRS*
(billion dollars, saar)

* Excluding Inventory Valuation Adjustment and Capital Consumption Adjustment.
Note: Shaded areas are recessions according to the National Bureau of Economic Research.
Source: Bureau of Labor Statistics and Bureau of Economic Analysis.

Figure 4.

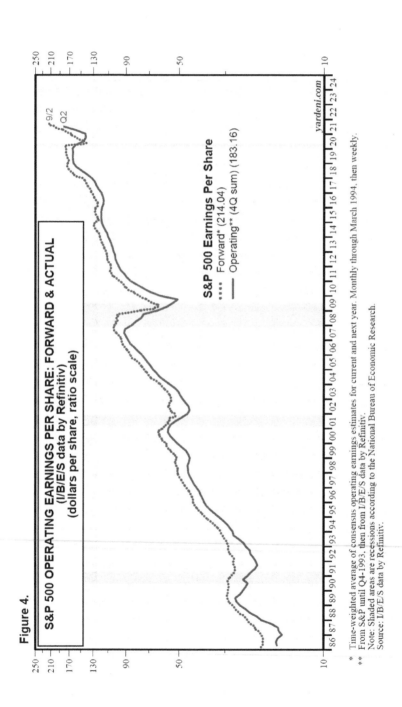

S&P 500 OPERATING EARNINGS PER SHARE: FORWARD & ACTUAL
(I/B/E/S data by Refinitiv)
(dollars per share, ratio scale)

S&P 500 Earnings Per Share
•••• Forward* (214.04)
—— Operating** (4Q sum) (183.16)

yardeni.com

* Time-weighted average of consensus operating earnings estimates for current and next year. Monthly through March 1994, then weekly.
** From S&P until Q4-1993, then from I/B/E/S data by Refinitiv.
Note: Shaded areas are recessions according to the National Bureau of Economic Research.
Source: I/B/E/S data by Refinitiv.

Figure 5.

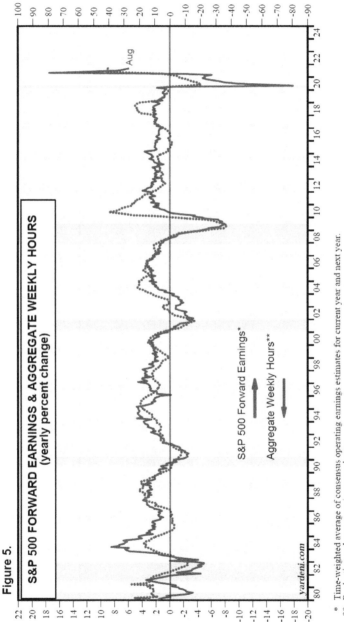

S&P 500 FORWARD EARNINGS & AGGREGATE WEEKLY HOURS
(yearly percent change)

S&P 500 Forward Earnings*

Aggregate Weekly Hours**

Aug

yardeni.com

* Time-weighted average of consensus operating earnings estimates for current year and next year.
** Production and nonsupervisory employees.
Note: Shaded areas are recessions according to the National Bureau of Economic Research.
Source: Bureau of Labor Statistics and Thomson Reuters I/B/E/S.

Figure 6.

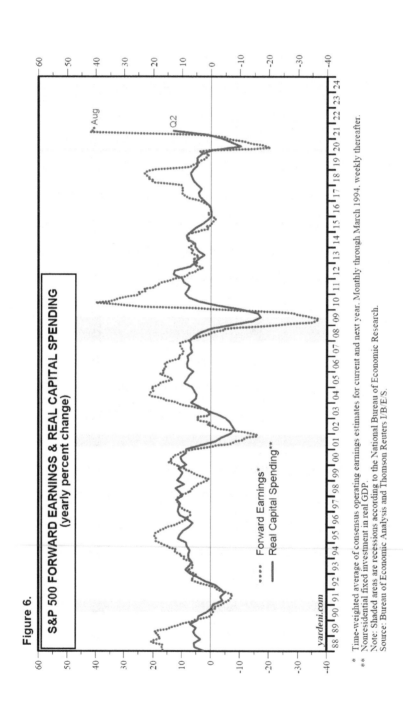

S&P 500 FORWARD EARNINGS & REAL CAPITAL SPENDING
(yearly percent change)

···· Forward Earnings*
—— Real Capital Spending**

yardeni.com

*   Time-weighted average of consensus operating earnings estimates for current and next year. Monthly through March 1994, weekly thereafter.
** Nonresidential fixed investment in real GDP.
Note: Shaded areas are recessions according to the National Bureau of Economic Research.
Source: Bureau of Economic Analysis and Thomson Reuters I/B/E/S.

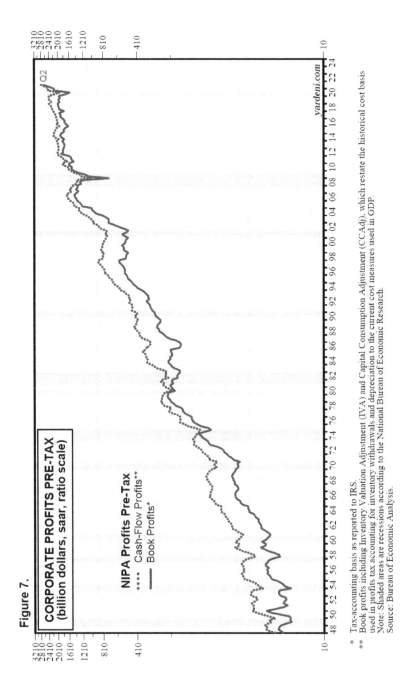

Figure 7.

CORPORATE PROFITS PRE-TAX
(billion dollars, saar, ratio scale)

NIPA Profits Pre-Tax
···· Cash-Flow Profits**
— Book Profits*

yardeni.com

* Tax-accounting basis as reported to IRS.
** Book profits including Inventory Valuation Adjustment (IVA) and Capital Consumption Adjustment (CCAdj), which restate the historical cost basis
used in profits tax accounting for inventory withdrawals and depreciation to the current cost measures used in GDP.
Note: Shaded areas are recessions according to the National Bureau of Economic Research.
Source: Bureau of Economic Analysis.

Figure 8.

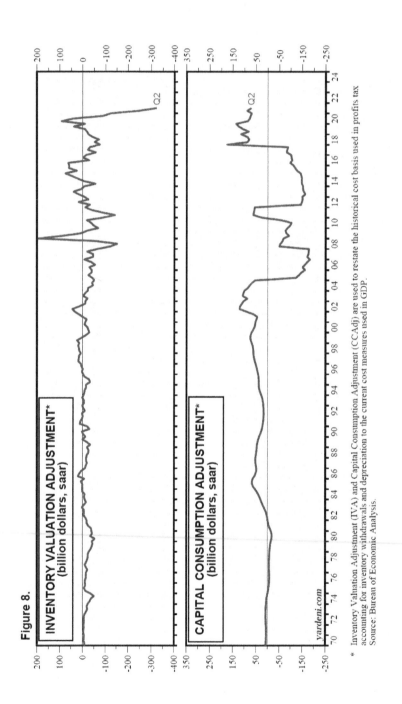

* Inventory Valuation Adjustment (IVA) and Capital Consumption Adjustment (CCAdj) are used to restate the historical cost basis used in profits tax accounting for inventory withdrawals and depreciation to the current cost measures used in GDP.
Source: Bureau of Economic Analysis.

Figure 9.

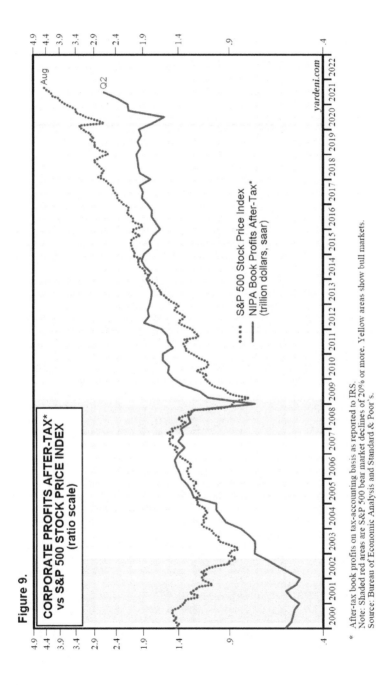

CORPORATE PROFITS AFTER-TAX*
vs S&P 500 STOCK PRICE INDEX
(ratio scale)

····· S&P 500 Stock Price Index

——— NIPA Book Profits After-Tax*
(trillion dollars, saar)

* After-tax book profits on tax-accounting basis as reported to IRS.
Note: Shaded red areas are S&P 500 bear market declines of 20% or more. Yellow areas show bull markets.
Source: Bureau of Economic Analysis and Standard & Poor's.

yardeni.com

Figure 10.

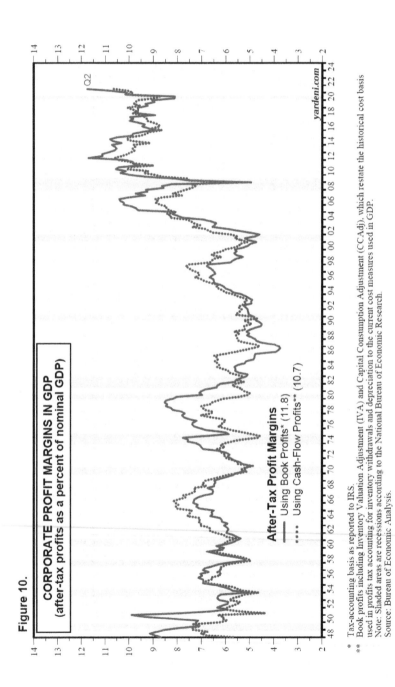

CORPORATE PROFIT MARGINS IN GDP
(after-tax profits as a percent of nominal GDP)

After-Tax Profit Margins
—— Using Book Profits* (11.8)
····· Using Cash-Flow Profits** (10.7)

yardeni.com

*   Tax-accounting basis as reported to IRS.
** Book profits including Inventory Valuation Adjustment (IVA) and Capital Consumption Adjustment (CCAdj), which restate the historical cost basis
    used in profits tax accounting for inventory withdrawals and depreciation to the current cost measures used in GDP.
Note: Shaded areas are recessions according to the National Bureau of Economic Research.
Source: Bureau of Economic Analysis.

Figure 11.

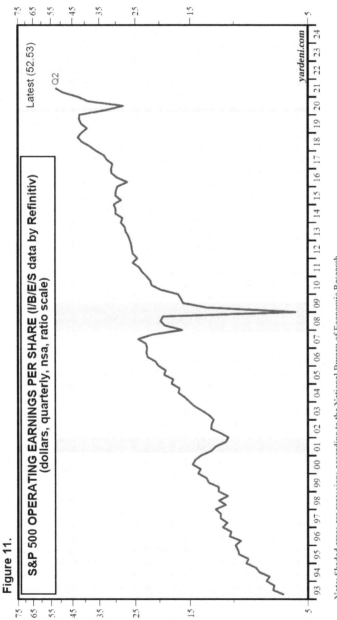

S&P 500 OPERATING EARNINGS PER SHARE (I/B/E/S data by Refinitiv)
(dollars, quarterly, nsa, ratio scale)

Latest (52.53)

Q2

yardeni.com

Note: Shaded areas are recessions according to the National Bureau of Economic Research.
Source: I/B/E/S data by Refinitiv.

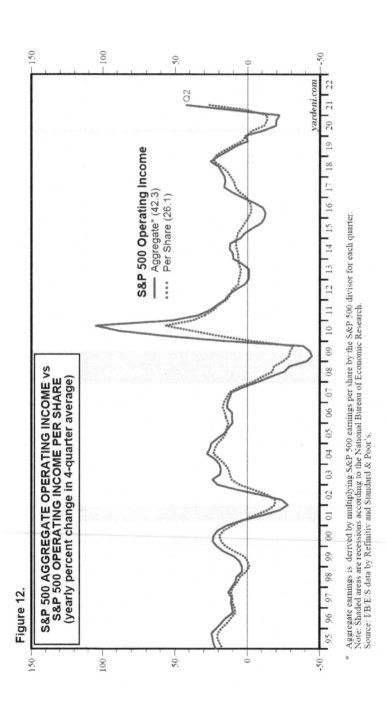

Figure 12.

**S&P 500 AGGREGATE OPERATING INCOME vs
S&P 500 OPERATING INCOME PER SHARE
(yearly percent change in 4-quarter average)**

S&P 500 Operating Income
— Aggregate* (42.3)
···· Per Share (26.1)

Q2

yardeni.com

* Aggregate earnings is derived by multiplying S&P 500 earnings per share by the S&P 500 divisor for each quarter.
Note: Shaded areas are recessions according to the National Bureau of Economic Research.
Source: I/B/E/S data by Refinitiv and Standard & Poor's.

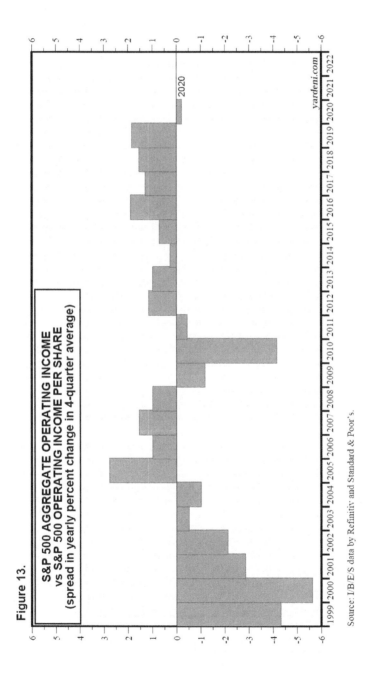

Figure 13.

S&P 500 AGGREGATE OPERATING INCOME
vs S&P 500 OPERATING INCOME PER SHARE
(spread in yearly percent change in 4-quarter average)

Source: I/B/E/S data by Refinitiv and Standard & Poor's.

Figure 14.

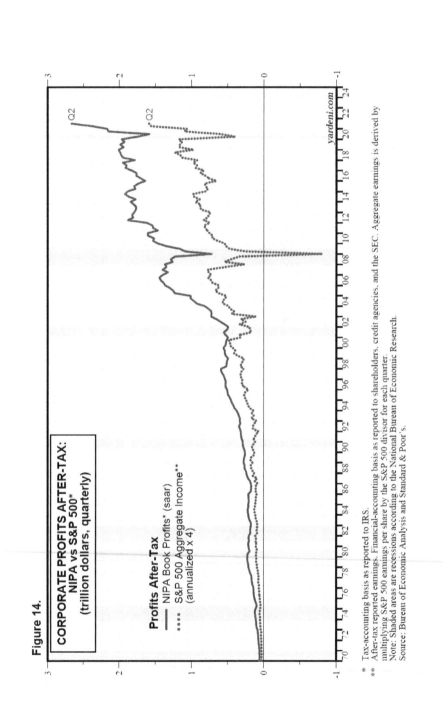

CORPORATE PROFITS AFTER-TAX:
NIPA vs S&P 500*
(trillion dollars, quarterly)

Profits After-Tax
—— NIPA Book Profits* (saar)
•••• S&P 500 Aggregate Income**
(annualized x 4)

yardeni.com

* Tax-accounting basis as reported to IRS.
** After-tax reported earnings. Financial-accounting basis as reported to shareholders, credit agencies, and the SEC. Aggregate earnings is derived by
multiplying S&P 500 earnings per share by the S&P 500 divisor for each quarter.
Note: Shaded areas are recessions according to the National Bureau of Economic Research.
Source: Bureau of Economic Analysis and Standard & Poor's.

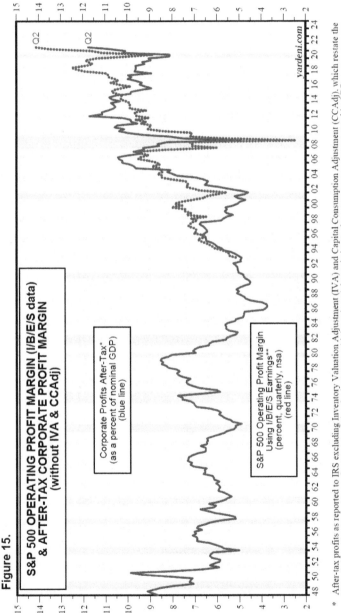

Figure 15.

S&P 500 OPERATING PROFIT MARGIN (I/B/E/S data) & AFTER-TAX CORPORATE PROFIT MARGIN (without IVA & CCAdj)

Corporate Profits After-Tax* (as a percent of nominal GDP) (blue line)

S&P 500 Operating Profit Margin Using I/B/E/S Earnings** (percent, quarterly, nsa) (red line)

yardeni.com

* After-tax profits as reported to IRS excluding Inventory Valuation Adjustment (IVA) and Capital Consumption Adjustment (CCAdj), which restate the historical cost basis used in profits tax accounting for inventory withdrawals and depreciation to the current cost measures used in GDP.

** Operating Profit Margin derived using revenues from S&P and earnings from I/B/E/S data by Refinitiv.

Note: Shaded areas are recessions according to the National Bureau of Economic Research.

Source: Standard & Poor's, Bureau of Economic Analysis, and I/B/E/S data by Refinitiv.

Figure 16.

NATIONAL INCOME SHARE:
CORPORATE PROFITS FROM CURRENT PRODUCTION PRE-TAX*
(as percent of National Income)

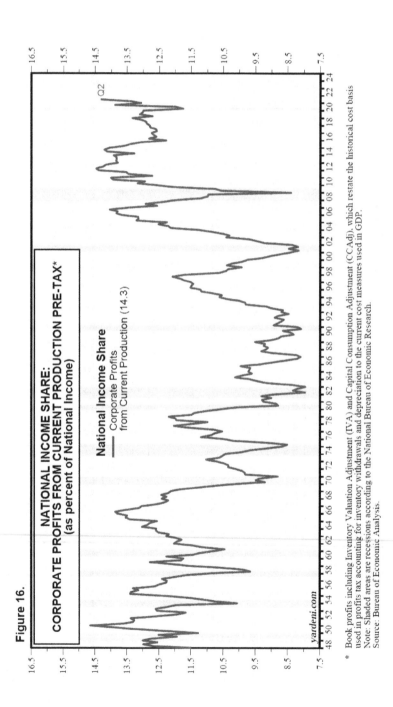

National Income Share
— Corporate Profits
from Current Production (14.3)

yardeni.com

* Book profits including Inventory Valuation Adjustment (IVA) and Capital Consumption Adjustment (CCAdj), which restate the historical cost basis used in profits tax accounting for inventory withdrawals and depreciation to the current cost measures used in GDP.
Note: Shaded areas are recessions according to the National Bureau of Economic Research.
Source: Bureau of Economic Analysis.

Figure 17.

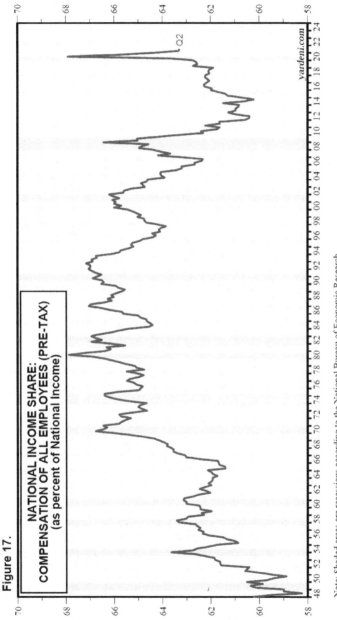

NATIONAL INCOME SHARE:
COMPENSATION OF ALL EMPLOYEES (PRE-TAX)
(as percent of National Income)

Note: Shaded areas are recessions according to the National Bureau of Economic Research.
Source: Bureau of Economic Analysis.

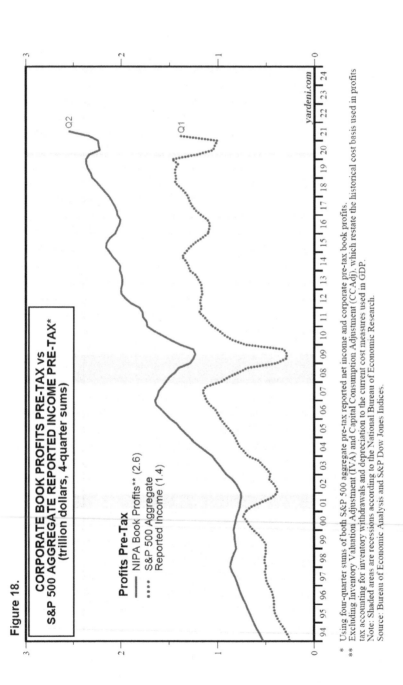

Figure 18.

CORPORATE BOOK PROFITS PRE-TAX vs
S&P 500 AGGREGATE REPORTED INCOME PRE-TAX*
(trillion dollars, 4-quarter sums)

Profits Pre-Tax
—— NIPA Book Profits** (2.6)
•••• S&P 500 Aggregate
     Reported Income (1.4)

*   Using four-quarter sums of both S&P 500 aggregate pre-tax reported net income and corporate pre-tax book profits.
** Excluding Inventory Valuation Adjustment (IVA) and Capital Consumption Adjustment (CCAdj), which restate the historical cost basis used in profits
    tax accounting for inventory withdrawals and depreciation to the current cost measures used in GDP.
    Note: Shaded areas are recessions according to the National Bureau of Economic Research.
    Source: Bureau of Economic Analysis and S&P Dow Jones Indices.

Figure 19.

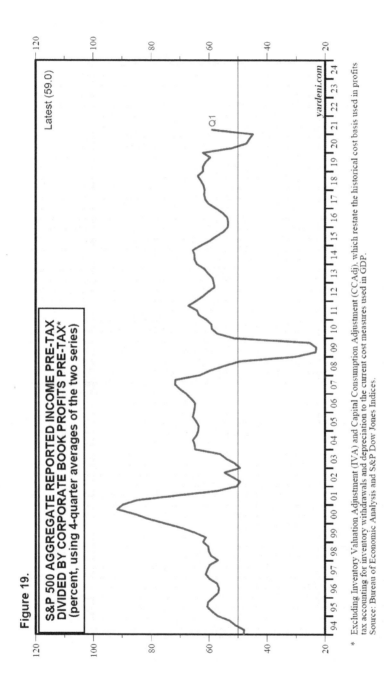

S&P 500 AGGREGATE REPORTED INCOME PRE-TAX DIVIDED BY CORPORATE BOOK PROFITS PRE-TAX* (percent, using 4-quarter averages of the two series)

* Excluding Inventory Valuation Adjustment (IVA) and Capital Consumption Adjustment (CCAdj), which restate the historical cost basis used in profits tax accounting for inventory withdrawals and depreciation to the current cost measures used in GDP.
Source: Bureau of Economic Analysis and S&P Dow Jones Indices.

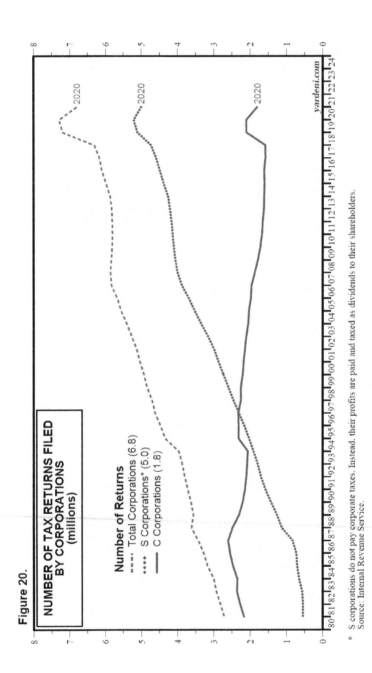

Figure 20.

NUMBER OF TAX RETURNS FILED BY CORPORATIONS
(millions)

Number of Returns
- - - Total Corporations (6.8)
····· S Corporations* (5.0)
—— C Corporations (1.8)

yardeni.com

* S corporations do not pay corporate taxes. Instead, their profits are paid and taxed as dividends to their shareholders.
Source: Internal Revenue Service.

Figure 21.

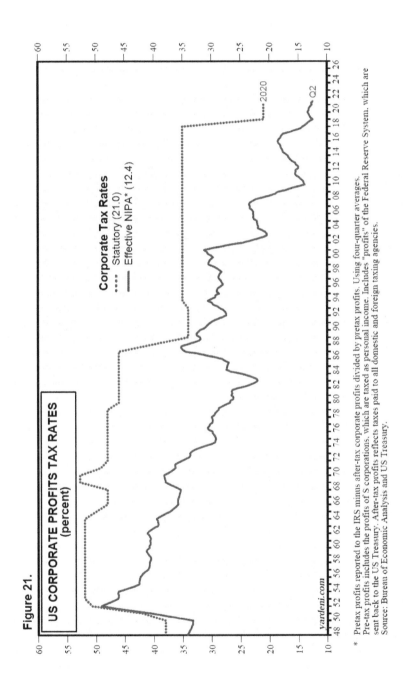

US CORPORATE PROFITS TAX RATES
(percent)

Corporate Tax Rates
•••• Statutory (21.0)
—— Effective NIPA* (12.4)

yardeni.com

* Pretax profits reported to the IRS minus after-tax corporate profits divided by pretax profits. Using four-quarter averages. Pre-tax profits includes the profits of S corporations, which are taxed as personal income. Includes "profits" of the Federal Reserve System, which are sent back to the US Treasury. After-tax profits reflects taxes paid to all domestic and foreign taxing agencies.
Source: Bureau of Economic Analysis and US Treasury.

Figure 22.

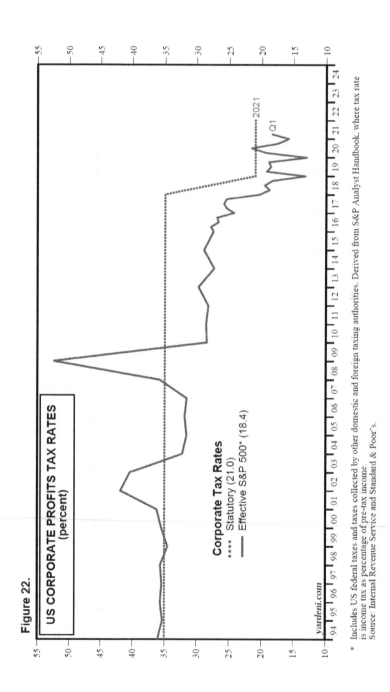

US CORPORATE PROFITS TAX RATES
(percent)

Corporate Tax Rates
•••• Statutory (21.0)
—— Effective S&P 500* (18.4)

yardeni.com

* Includes US federal taxes and taxes collected by other domestic and foreign taxing authorities. Derived from S&P Analyst Handbook. where tax rate
is income tax as percentage of pre-tax income.
Source: Internal Revenue Service and Standard & Poor's.

Figure 23.

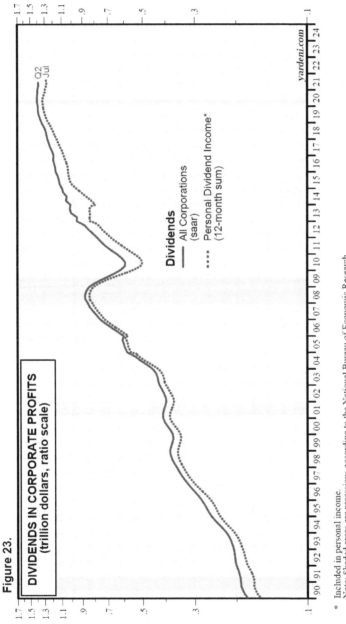

DIVIDENDS IN CORPORATE PROFITS
(trillion dollars, ratio scale)

Dividends
— All Corporations
(saar)
••• Personal Dividend Income*
(12-month sum)

yardeni.com

* Included in personal income.
Note: Shaded areas are recessions according to the National Bureau of Economic Research.
Source: Bureau of Economic Analysis.

Figure 24.

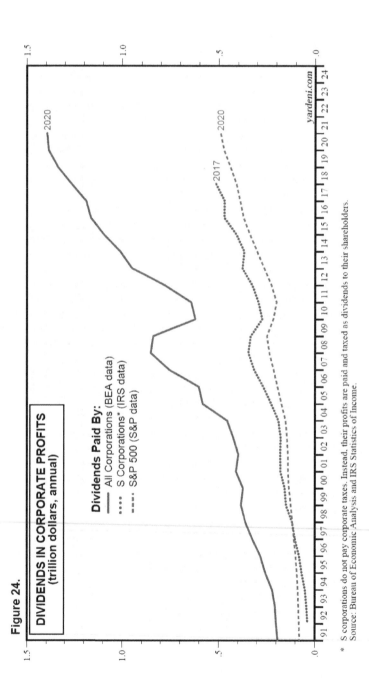

DIVIDENDS IN CORPORATE PROFITS
(trillion dollars, annual)

Dividends Paid By:
— All Corporations (BEA data)
····· S Corporations* (IRS data)
– – S&P 500 (S&P data)

yardeni.com

* S corporations do not pay corporate taxes. Instead, their profits are paid and taxed as dividends to their shareholders.
Source: Bureau of Economic Analysis and IRS Statistics of Income.

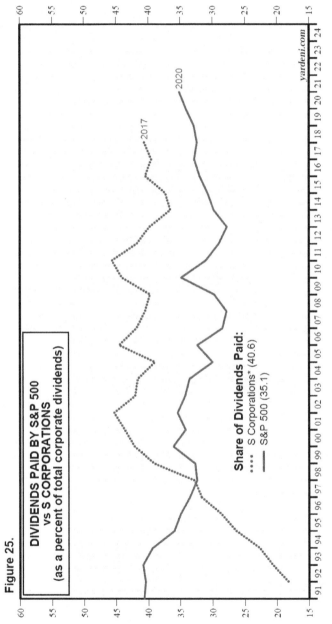

Figure 25.

DIVIDENDS PAID BY S&P 500
vs S CORPORATIONS
(as a percent of total corporate dividends)

Share of Dividends Paid:
···· S Corporations* (40.6)
—— S&P 500 (35.1)

2017

2020

yardeni.com

* S corporations do not pay corporate taxes. Instead, their profits are paid and taxed as dividends to their shareholders.
Source: Bureau of Economic Analysis and IRS Statistics of Income.

Figure 26.

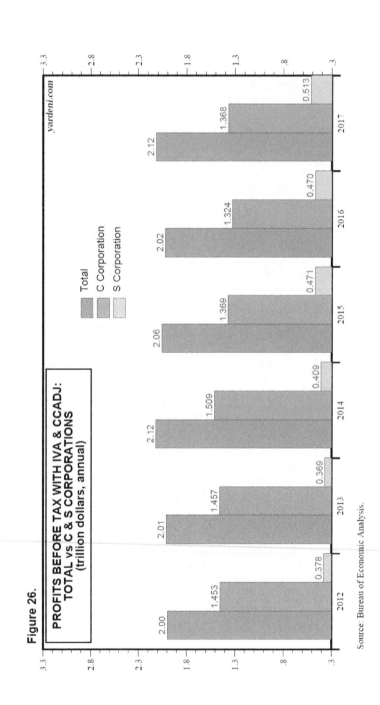

PROFITS BEFORE TAX WITH IVA & CCADJ:
TOTAL vs C & S CORPORATIONS
(trillion dollars, annual)

Total
C Corporation
S Corporation

yardeni.com

Source: Bureau of Economic Analysis.

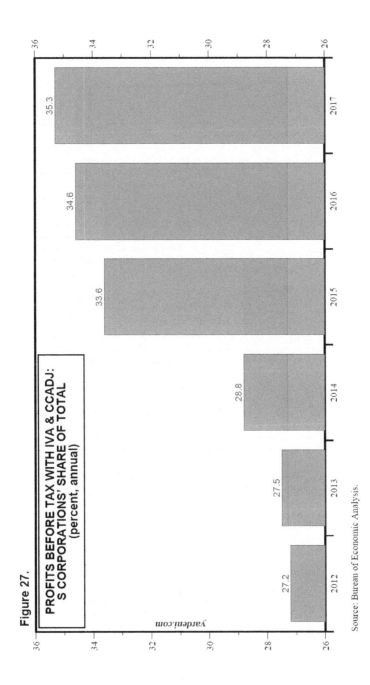

Figure 27.

PROFITS BEFORE TAX WITH IVA & CCADJ:
S CORPORATIONS' SHARE OF TOTAL
(percent, annual)

Source: Bureau of Economic Analysis.

Figure 28.

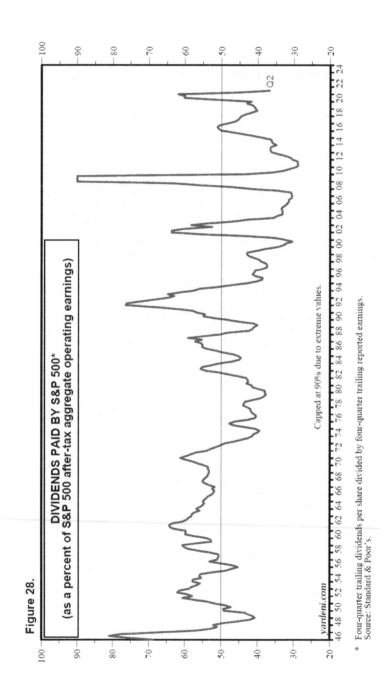

DIVIDENDS PAID BY S&P 500*
(as a percent of S&P 500 after-tax aggregate operating earnings)

yardeni.com

Capped at 90% due to extreme values.

* Four-quarter trailing dividends per share divided by four-quarter trailing reported earnings.
Source: Standard & Poor's.

Figure 29.

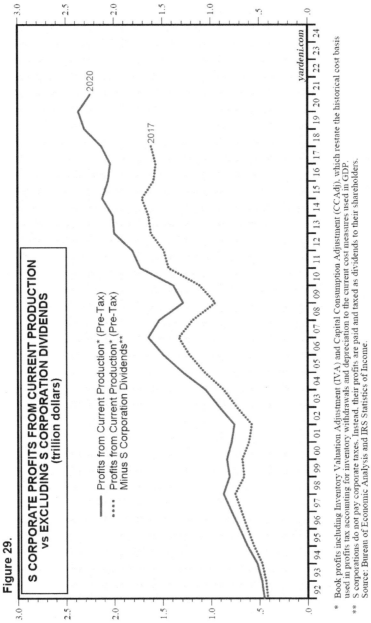

S CORPORATE PROFITS FROM CURRENT PRODUCTION
vs EXCLUDING S CORPORATION DIVIDENDS
(trillion dollars)

—— Profits from Current Production* (Pre-Tax)
···· Profits from Current Production* (Pre-Tax)
     Minus S Corporation Dividends**

* Book profits including Inventory Valuation Adjustment (IVA) and Capital Consumption Adjustment (CCAdj), which restate the historical cost basis used in profits tax accounting for inventory withdrawals and depreciation to the current cost measures used in GDP.

** S corporations do not pay corporate taxes. Instead, their profits are paid and taxed as dividends to their shareholders.
     Source: Bureau of Economic Analysis and IRS Statistics of Income.

Figure 30.

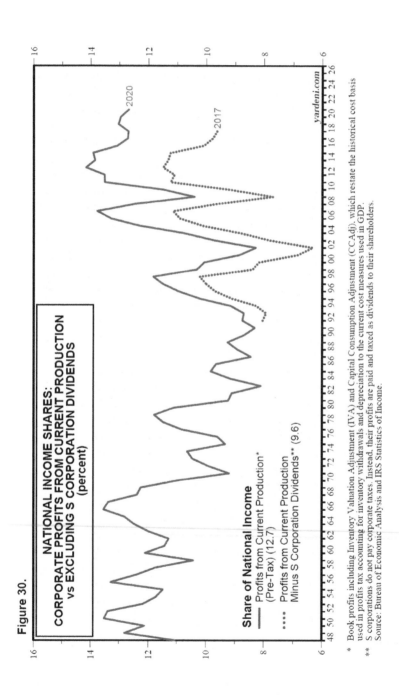

NATIONAL INCOME SHARES:
CORPORATE PROFITS FROM CURRENT PRODUCTION
vs EXCLUDING S CORPORATION DIVIDENDS
(percent)

Share of National Income
— Profits from Current Production*
  (Pre-Tax) (12.7)

···· Profits from Current Production
  Minus S Corporation Dividends** (9.6)

yardeni.com

* Book profits including Inventory Valuation Adjustment (IVA) and Capital Consumption Adjustment (CCAdj), which restate the historical cost basis used in profits tax accounting for inventory withdrawals and depreciation to the current cost measures used in GDP.
** S corporations do not pay corporate taxes. Instead, their profits are paid and taxed as dividends to their shareholders.
Source: Bureau of Economic Analysis and IRS Statistics of Income.

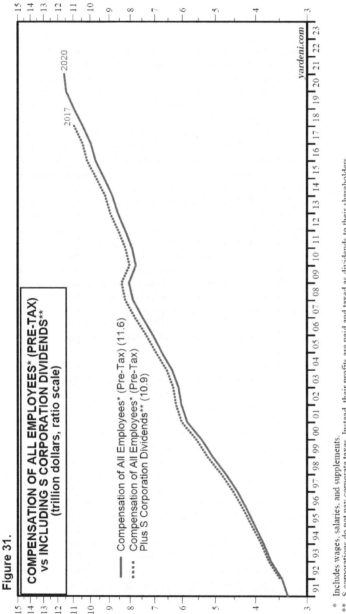

Figure 31.

COMPENSATION OF ALL EMPLOYEES* (PRE-TAX) vs INCLUDING S CORPORATION DIVIDENDS**
(trillion dollars, ratio scale)

— Compensation of All Employees* (Pre-Tax) (11.6)
···· Compensation of All Employees* (Pre-Tax) Plus S Corporation Dividends** (10.9)

* Includes wages, salaries, and supplements.
** S corporations do not pay corporate taxes. Instead, their profits are paid and taxed as dividends to their shareholders.
  Source: Bureau of Economic Analysis and IRS Statistics of Income.

yardeni.com

Figure 32.

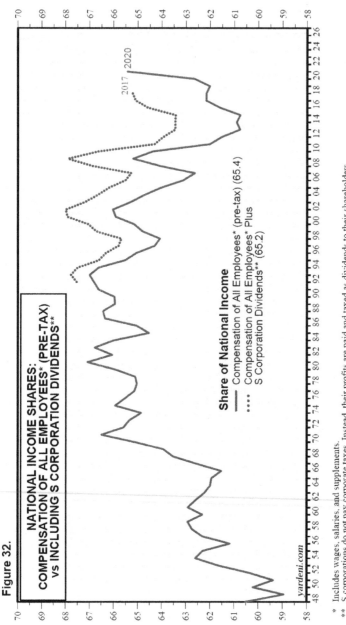

NATIONAL INCOME SHARES:
COMPENSATION OF ALL EMPLOYEES* (PRE-TAX)
vs INCLUDING S CORPORATION DIVIDENDS**

Share of National Income
— Compensation of All Employees* (pre-tax) (65.4)
···· Compensation of All Employees* Plus
    S Corporation Dividends** (65.2)

yardeni.com

* Includes wages, salaries, and supplements.
** S corporations do not pay corporate taxes. Instead, their profits are paid and taxed as dividends to their shareholders.
Source: Bureau of Economic Analysis and IRS Statistics of Income.

Figure 33.

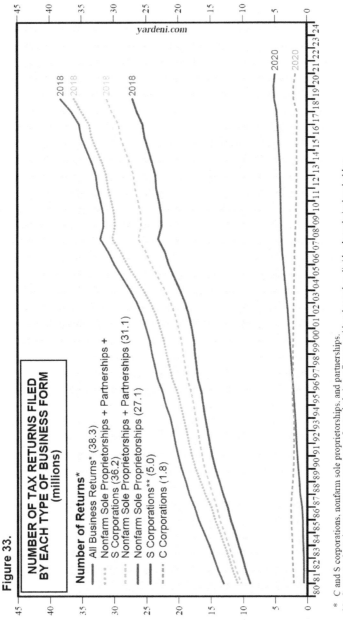

NUMBER OF TAX RETURNS FILED
BY EACH TYPE OF BUSINESS FORM
(millions)

Number of Returns*

—— All Business Returns* (38.3)
········· Nonfarm Sole Proprietorships + Partnerships +
S Corporations (36.2)
– – – Nonfarm Sole Proprietorships + Partnerships (31.1)
—— Nonfarm Sole Proprietorships (27.1)
—— S Corporations** (5.0)
– – – C Corporations (1.8)

*   C and S corporations. nonfarm sole proprietorships. and partnerships.
** S corporations do not pay corporate taxes. Instead. their profits are paid and taxed as dividends to their shareholders.
Source: Internal Revenue Service.

yardeni.com

Figure 34.

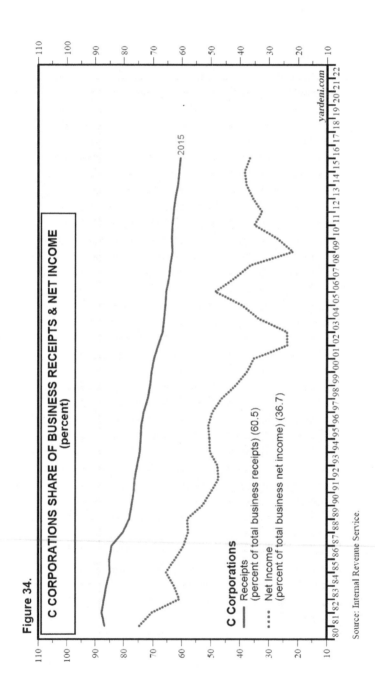

C CORPORATIONS SHARE OF BUSINESS RECEIPTS & NET INCOME
(percent)

C Corporations
— Receipts
(percent of total business receipts) (60.5)
···· Net Income
(percent of total business net income) (36.7)

Source: Internal Revenue Service.

yardeni.com

Figure 35.

NET INCOME BY EACH TYPE OF
BUSINESS FORM
(trillion dollars)

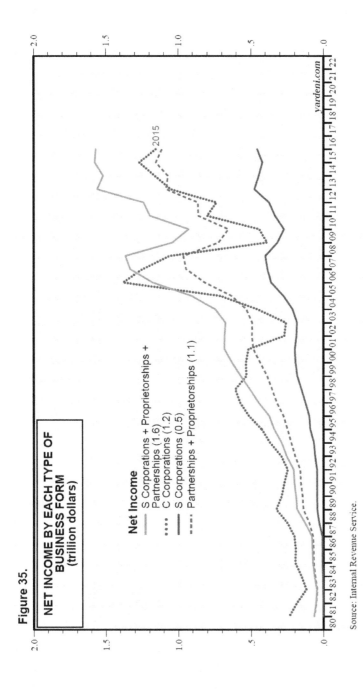

Net Income

—— S Corporations + Proprietorships +
        Partnerships (1.6)
····· C Corporations (1.2)
—— S Corporations (0.5)
- - - Partnerships + Proprietorships (1.1)

Source: Internal Revenue Service.

Figure 36.

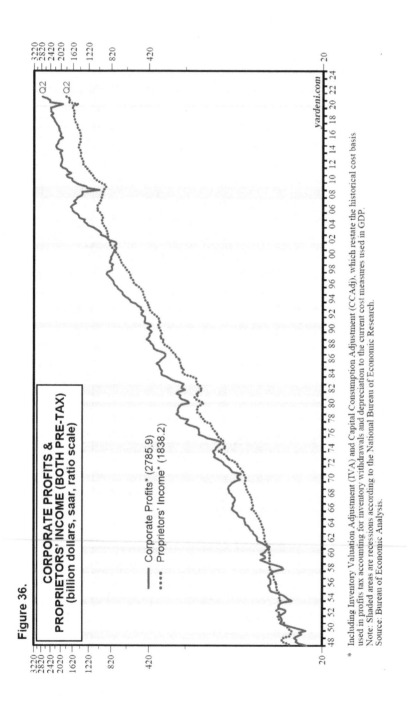

CORPORATE PROFITS &
PROPRIETORS' INCOME (BOTH PRE-TAX)
(billion dollars, saar, ratio scale)

—— Corporate Profits* (2785.9)
····· Proprietors' Income* (1838.2)

yardeni.com

* Including Inventory Valuation Adjustment (IVA) and Capital Consumption Adjustment (CCAdj), which restate the historical cost basis
used in profits tax accounting for inventory withdrawals and depreciation to the current cost measures used in GDP.
Note: Shaded areas are recessions according to the National Bureau of Economic Research.
Source: Bureau of Economic Analysis.

Figure 37.

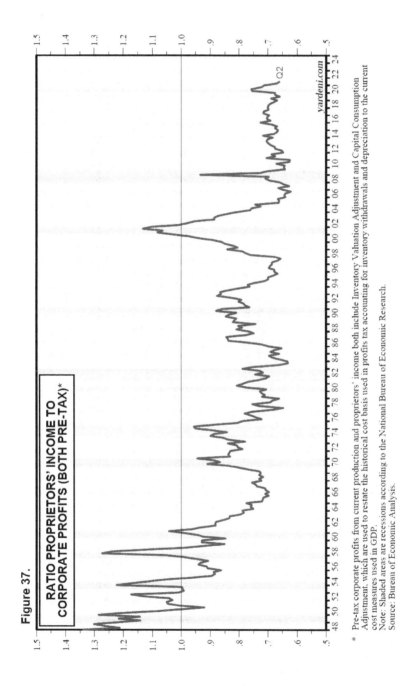

RATIO PROPRIETORS' INCOME TO
CORPORATE PROFITS (BOTH PRE-TAX)*

yardeni.com

* Pre-tax corporate profits from current production and proprietors' income both include Inventory Valuation Adjustment and Capital Consumption
Adjustment, which are used to restate the historical cost basis used in profits tax accounting for inventory withdrawals and depreciation to the current
cost measures used in GDP.
Note: Shaded areas are recessions according to the National Bureau of Economic Research.
Source: Bureau of Economic Analysis.

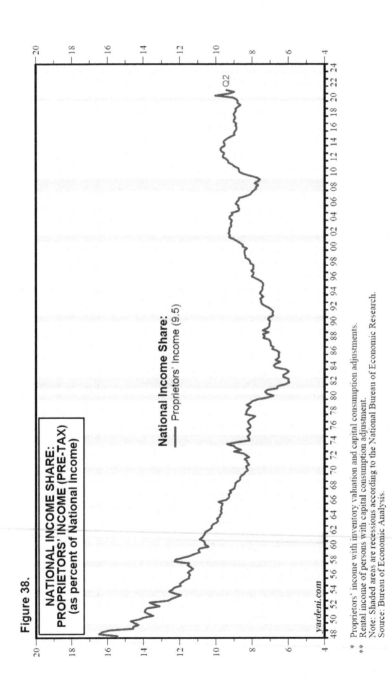

Figure 38.

**NATIONAL INCOME SHARE:
PROPRIETORS' INCOME (PRE-TAX)
(as percent of National Income)**

National Income Share:
—— Proprietors' Income (9.5)

yardeni.com

*   Proprietors' income with inventory valuation and capital consumption adjustments.
**   Rental income of persons with capital consumption adjustment.
Note: Shaded areas are recessions according to the National Bureau of Economic Research.
Source: Bureau of Economic Analysis.

Figure 39.

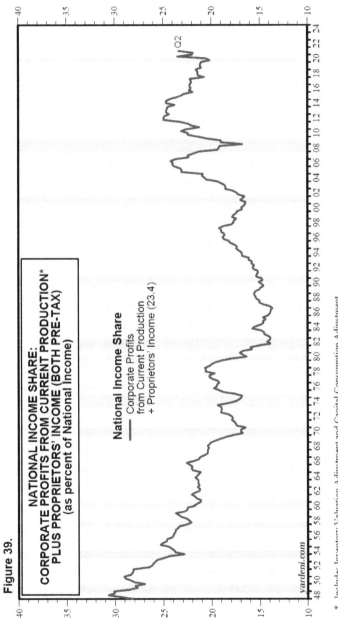

NATIONAL INCOME SHARE:
CORPORATE PROFITS FROM CURRENT PRODUCTION*
PLUS PROPRIETORS' INCOME (BOTH PRE-TAX)
(as percent of National Income)

National Income Share
— Corporate Profits
   from Current Production
   + Proprietors' Income (23.4)

yardeni.com

* Includes Inventory Valuation Adjustment and Capital Consumption Adjustment.
Note: Shaded areas are recessions according to the National Bureau of Economic Research.
Source: Bureau of Economic Analysis.

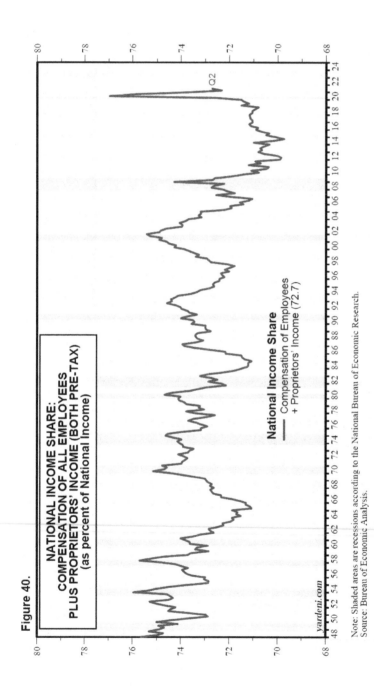

Figure 40.

NATIONAL INCOME SHARE:
COMPENSATION OF ALL EMPLOYEES
PLUS PROPRIETORS' INCOME (BOTH PRE-TAX)
(as percent of National Income)

National Income Share
— Compensation of Employees
   + Proprietors' Income (72.7)

yardeni.com

Note: Shaded areas are recessions according to the National Bureau of Economic Research.
Source: Bureau of Economic Analysis.

Figure 41.

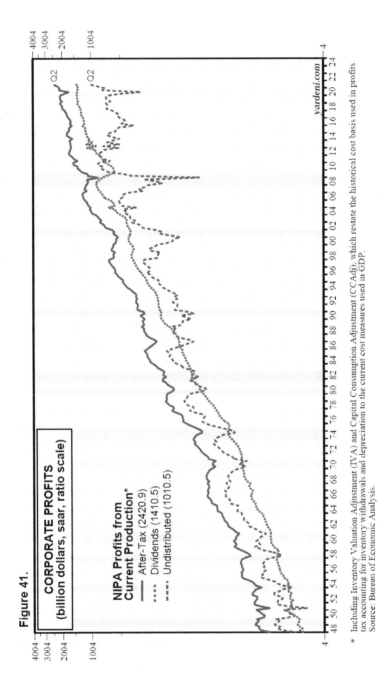

CORPORATE PROFITS
(billion dollars, saar, ratio scale)

NIPA Profits from
Current Production*
—— After-Tax (2420.9)
········ Dividends (1410.5)
– – – Undistributed (1010.5)

* Including Inventory Valuation Adjustment (IVA) and Capital Consumption Adjustment (CCAdj), which restate the historical cost basis used in profits tax accounting for inventory withdrawals and depreciation to the current cost measures used in GDP.
Source: Bureau of Economic Analysis.

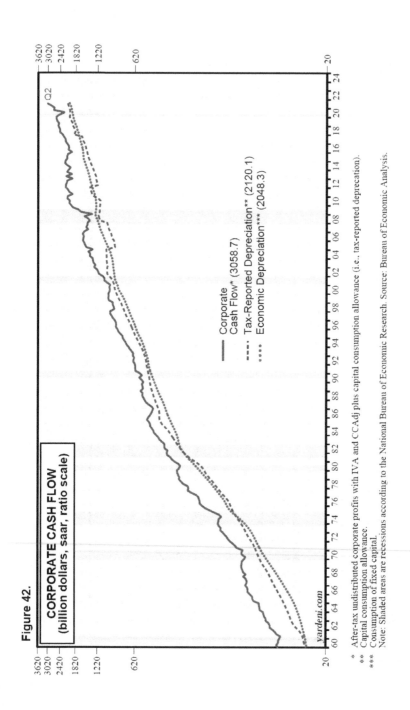

Figure 42.

CORPORATE CASH FLOW
(billion dollars, saar, ratio scale)

Corporate Cash Flow* (3058.7)
Tax-Reported Depreciation** (2120.1)
Economic Depreciation*** (2048.3)

*   After-tax undistributed corporate profits with IVA and CCAdj plus capital consumption allowance (i.e., tax-reported deprecation).
**   Capital consumption allowance.
***   Consumption of fixed capital.
Note: Shaded areas are recessions according to the National Bureau of Economic Research. Source: Bureau of Economic Analysis.

yardeni.com

Figure 43.

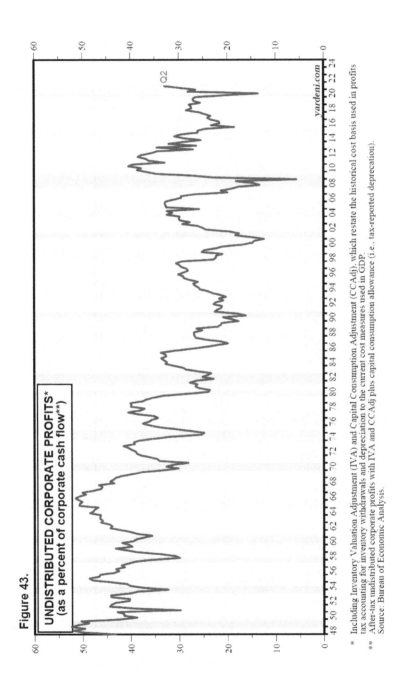

UNDISTRIBUTED CORPORATE PROFITS*
(as a percent of corporate cash flow**)

* Including Inventory Valuation Adjustment (IVA) and Capital Consumption Adjustment (CCAdj), which restate the historical cost basis used in profits tax accounting for inventory withdrawals and depreciation to the current cost measures used in GDP.
** After-tax undistributed corporate profits with IVA and CCAdj plus capital consumption allowance (i.e., tax-reported depreciation).
Source: Bureau of Economic Analysis.

yardeni.com

Figure 44.

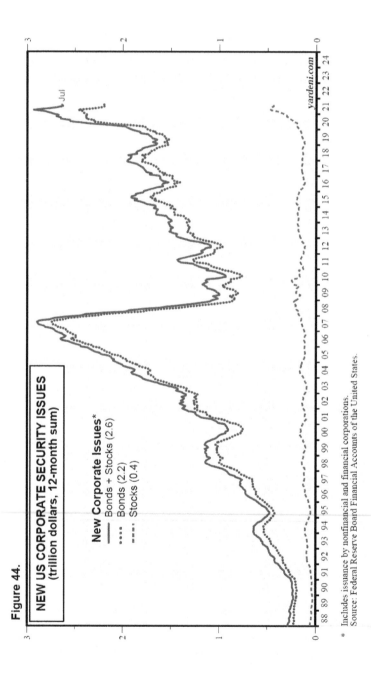

NEW US CORPORATE SECURITY ISSUES
(trillion dollars, 12-month sum)

New Corporate Issues*
— Bonds + Stocks (2.6)
···· Bonds (2.2)
---- Stocks (0.4)

* Includes issuance by nonfinancial and financial corporations.
Source: Federal Reserve Board Financial Accounts of the United States.

yardeni.com

Figure 45.

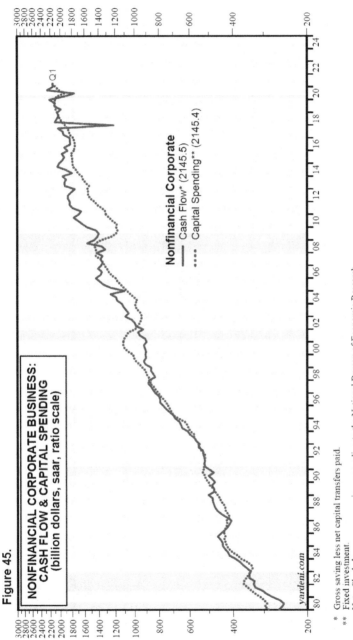

NONFINANCIAL CORPORATE BUSINESS:
CASH FLOW & CAPITAL SPENDING
(billion dollars, saar, ratio scale)

Nonfinancial Corporate
—— Cash Flow* (2145.5)
•••• Capital Spending** (2145.4)

*   Gross saving less net capital transfers paid.
** Fixed investment.
Note: Shaded areas are recessions according to the National Bureau of Economic Research.
Source: Federal Reserve Board.

yardeni.com

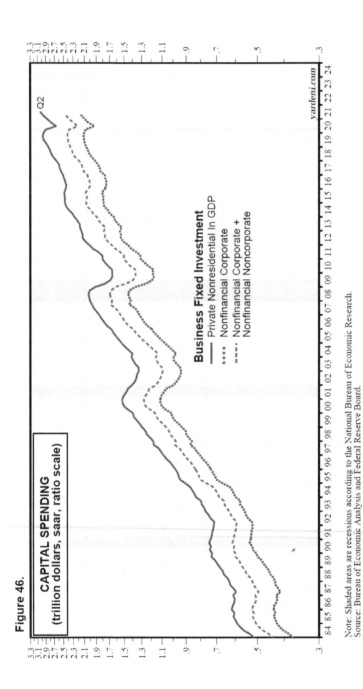

Figure 46.

Note: Shaded areas are recessions according to the National Bureau of Economic Research.
Source: Bureau of Economic Analysis and Federal Reserve Board.

Figure 47.

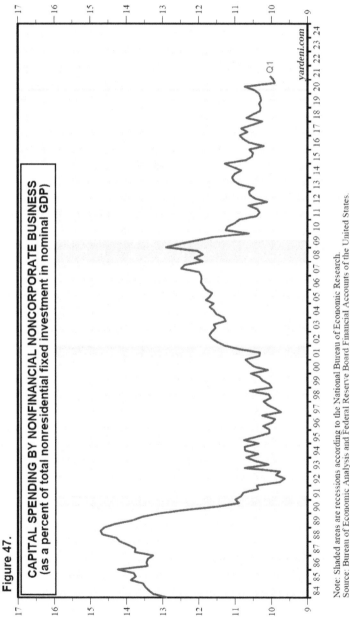

CAPITAL SPENDING BY NONFINANCIAL NONCORPORATE BUSINESS
(as a percent of total nonresidential fixed investment in nominal GDP)

Note: Shaded areas are recessions according to the National Bureau of Economic Research.
Source: Bureau of Economic Analysis and Federal Reserve Board Financial Accounts of the United States.

Figure 48.

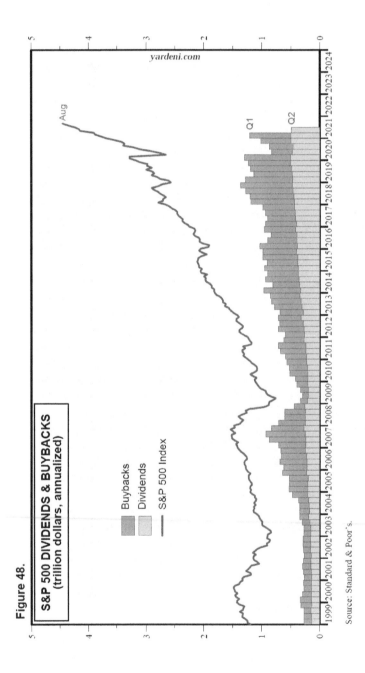

S&P 500 DIVIDENDS & BUYBACKS
(trillion dollars, annualized)

Buybacks
Dividends
—— S&P 500 Index

Source: Standard & Poor's.

Figure 49.

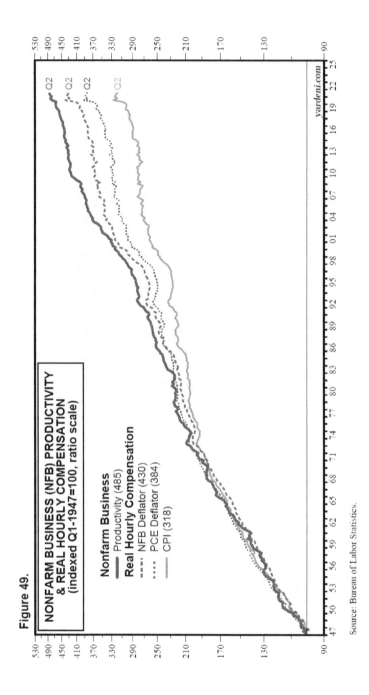

NONFARM BUSINESS (NFB) PRODUCTIVITY
& REAL HOURLY COMPENSATION
(indexed Q1-1947=100, ratio scale)

Nonfarm Business
— Productivity (485)
Real Hourly Compensation
-·-· NFB Deflator (430)
····· PCE Deflator (384)
— CPI (318)

Source: Bureau of Labor Statistics.

yardeni.com

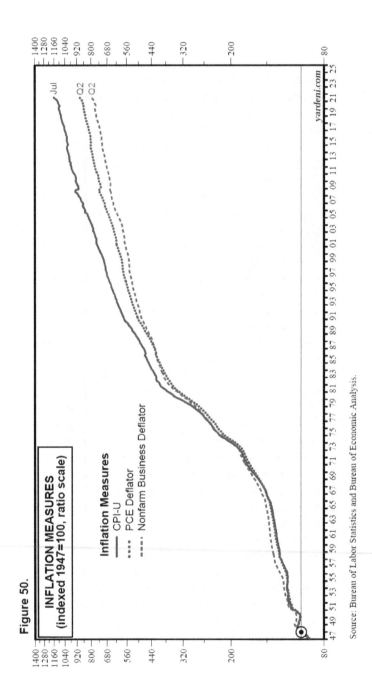

Figure 50.

INFLATION MEASURES
(indexed 1947=100, ratio scale)

Inflation Measures
— CPI-U
···· PCE Deflator
---- Nonfarm Business Deflator

Source: Bureau of Labor Statistics and Bureau of Economic Analysis.

yardeni.com

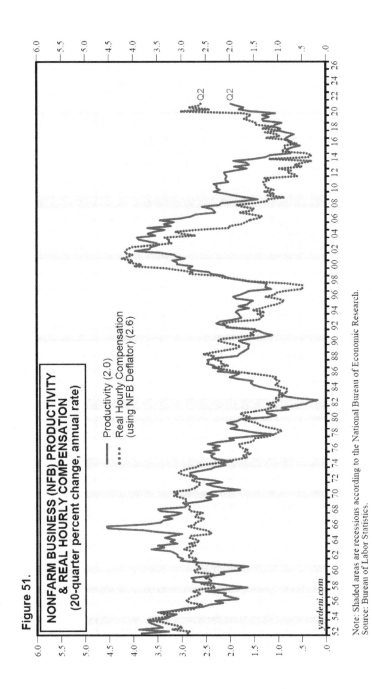

Figure 51.

NONFARM BUSINESS (NFB) PRODUCTIVITY
& REAL HOURLY COMPENSATION
(20-quarter percent change, annual rate)

—— Productivity (2.0)
•••• Real Hourly Compensation
       (using NFB Deflator) (2.6)

yardeni.com

Note: Shaded areas are recessions according to the National Bureau of Economic Research.
Source: Bureau of Labor Statistics.

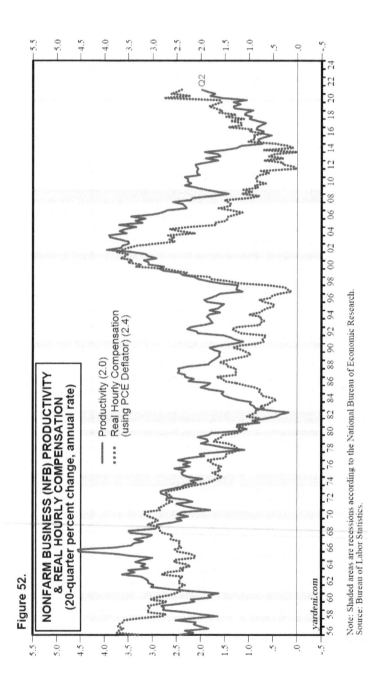

Figure 52.

NONFARM BUSINESS (NFB) PRODUCTIVITY & REAL HOURLY COMPENSATION
(20-quarter percent change, annual rate)

— Productivity (2.0)
···· Real Hourly Compensation
(using PCE Deflator) (2.4)

yardeni.com

Note: Shaded areas are recessions according to the National Bureau of Economic Research.
Source: Bureau of Labor Statistics.

Figure 53.

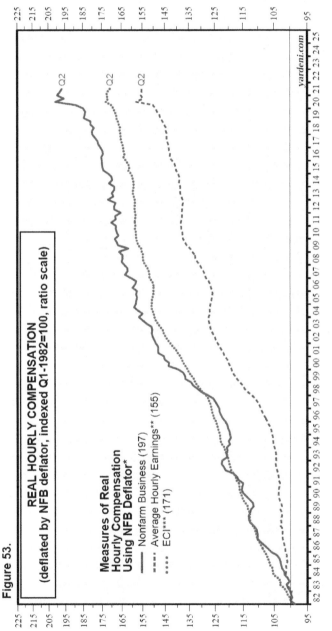

REAL HOURLY COMPENSATION
(deflated by NFB deflator, indexed Q1-1982=100, ratio scale)

**Measures of Real
Hourly Compensation
Using NFB Deflator***
—— Nonfarm Business (197)
- - - Average Hourly Earnings** (155)
····· ECI*** (171)

yardeni.com

*   Nonfarm Business Deflator.
**   Wages only of production and nonsupervisory workers.
*** Employment Cost Index including wages, salaries, and benefits in the private sector.
     Source: Bureau of Labor Statistics.

Figure 54.

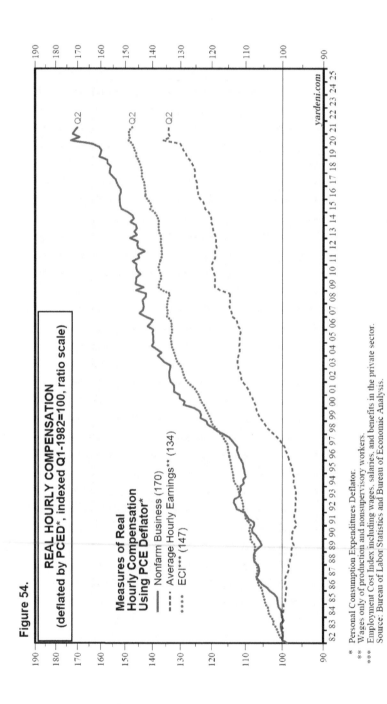

REAL HOURLY COMPENSATION
(defliated by PCED*, indexed Q1-1982=100, ratio scale)

Measures of Real
Hourly Compensation
Using PCE Deflator*
   — Nonfarm Business (170)
   ▪▪▪ Average Hourly Earnings** (134)
   •••• ECI*** (147)

yardeni.com

*   Personal Consumption Expenditures Deflator.
** Wages only of production and nonsupervisory workers.
*** Employment Cost Index including wages, salaries, and benefits in the private sector.
     Source: Bureau of Labor Statistics and Bureau of Economic Analysis.

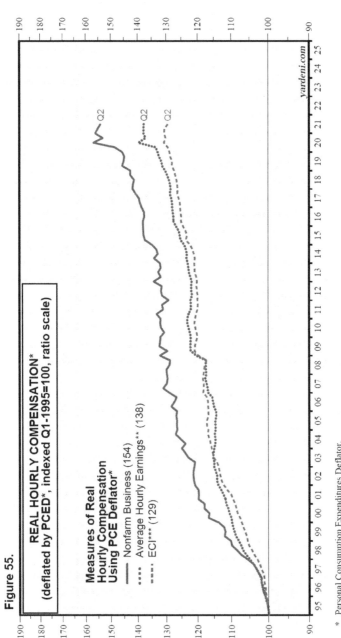

Figure 55.

REAL HOURLY COMPENSATION*
(deflated by PCED*, indexed Q1-1995=100, ratio scale)

Measures of Real
Hourly Compensation
Using PCE Deflator*
—— Nonfarm Business (154)
····· Average Hourly Earnings** (138)
–––– ECI*** (129)

*   Personal Consumption Expenditures Deflator.
**   Wages only of production and nonsupervisory workers.
*** Employment Cost Index including wages, salaries, and benefits in the private sector.
     Source: Bureau of Labor Statistics and Bureau of Economic Analysis.

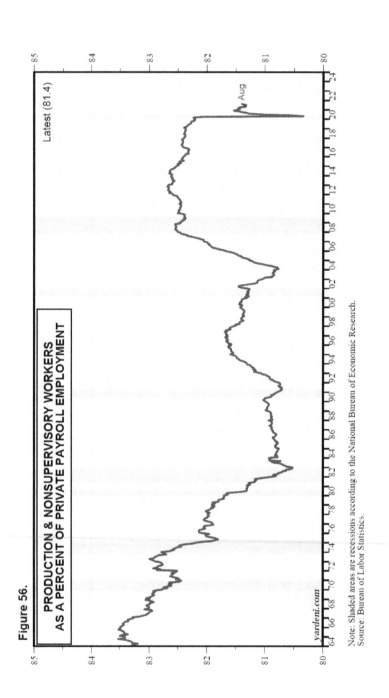

Figure 56.

PRODUCTION & NONSUPERVISORY WORKERS
AS A PERCENT OF PRIVATE PAYROLL EMPLOYMENT

Latest (81.4)

Aug

yardeni.com

Note: Shaded areas are recessions according to the National Bureau of Economic Research.
Source: Bureau of Labor Statistics.

Figure 57.

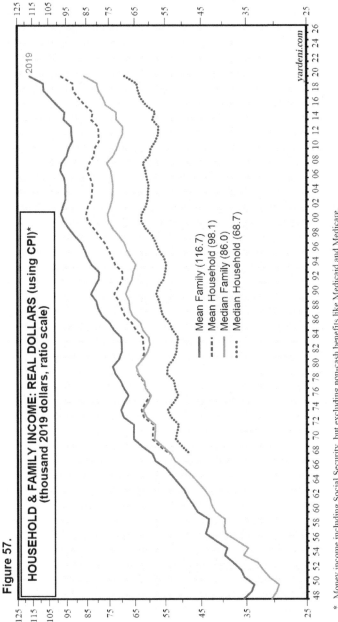

HOUSEHOLD & FAMILY INCOME: REAL DOLLARS (using CPI)*
(thousand 2019 dollars, ratio scale)

Mean Family (116.7)
Mean Household (98.1)
Median Family (86.0)
Median Household (68.7)

yardeni.com

* Money income including Social Security, but excluding non-cash benefits like Medicaid and Medicare.
Source: Census Bureau and Current Population Reports.

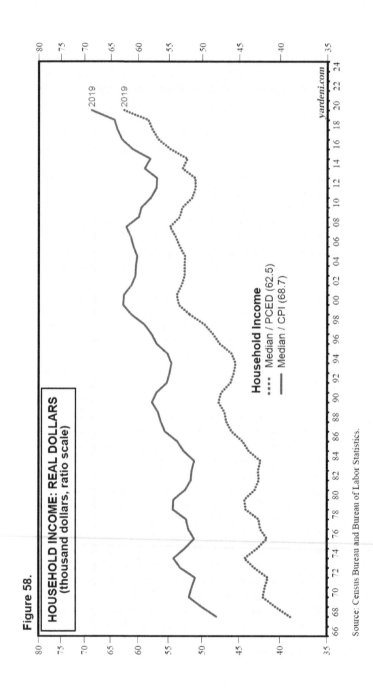

Figure 58.

HOUSEHOLD INCOME: REAL DOLLARS
(thousand dollars, ratio scale)

Household Income
···· Median / PCED (62.5)
— Median / CPI (68.7)

2019

2019

yardeni.com

Source: Census Bureau and Bureau of Labor Statistics.

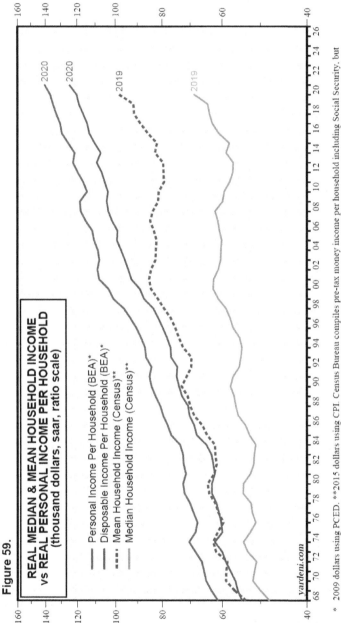

Figure 59.

**REAL MEDIAN & MEAN HOUSEHOLD INCOME
vs REAL PERSONAL INCOME PER HOUSEHOLD
(thousand dollars, saar, ratio scale)**

Personal Income Per Household (BEA)*
Disposable Income Per Household (BEA)*
Mean Household Income (Census)**
Median Household Income (Census)**

yardeni.com

* 2009 dollars using PCED. **2015 dollars using CPI. Census Bureau compiles pre-tax money income per household including Social Security, but excluding non-cash benefits like Medicaid and Medicare.
Source: Bureau of Economic Analysis, Census Bureau and Current Population Reports.

Figure 60.

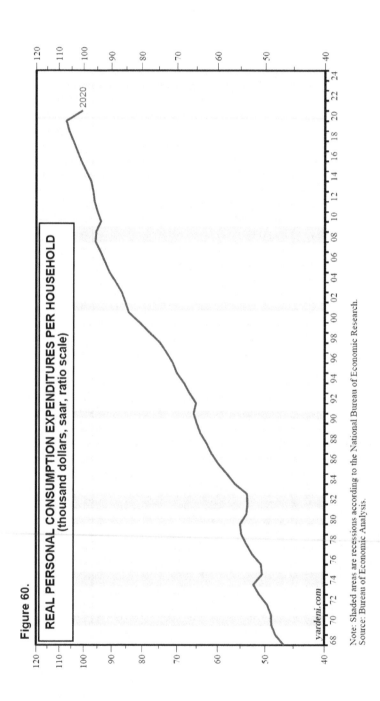

REAL PERSONAL CONSUMPTION EXPENDITURES PER HOUSEHOLD
(thousand dollars, saar, ratio scale)

yardeni.com

Note: Shaded areas are recessions according to the National Bureau of Economic Research.
Source: Bureau of Economic Analysis.

Figure 61.

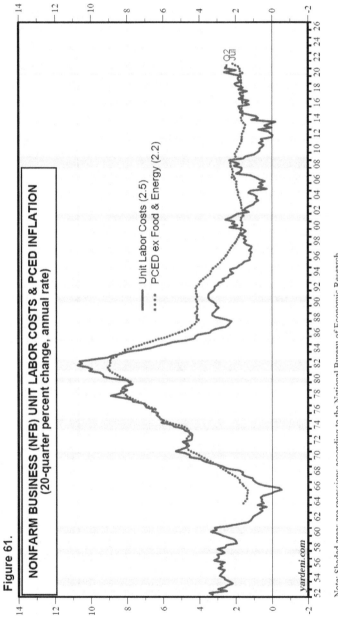

NONFARM BUSINESS (NFB) UNIT LABOR COSTS & PCED INFLATION
(20-quarter percent change, annual rate)

— Unit Labor Costs (2.5)
···· PCED ex Food & Energy (2.2)

yardeni.com

Note: Shaded areas are recessions according to the National Bureau of Economic Research.
Source: Bureau of Labor Statistics.

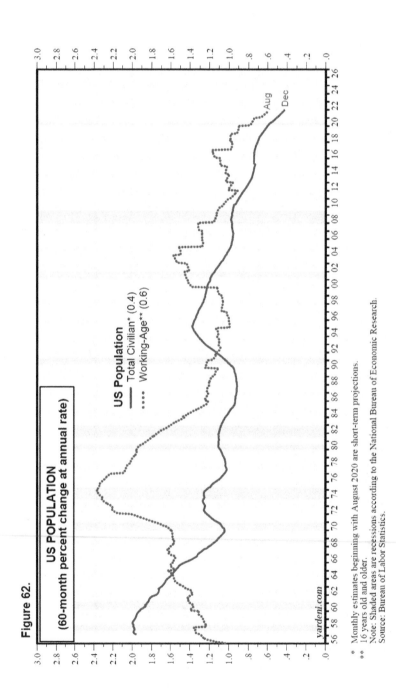

Figure 62.

US POPULATION
(60-month percent change at annual rate)

US Population
—— Total Civilian* (0.4)
••••• Working-Age** (0.6)

yardeni.com

* Monthly estimates beginning with August 2020 are short-term projections.
** 16 years old and older.
Note: Shaded areas are recessions according to the National Bureau of Economic Research.
Source: Bureau of Labor Statistics.

Figure 63.

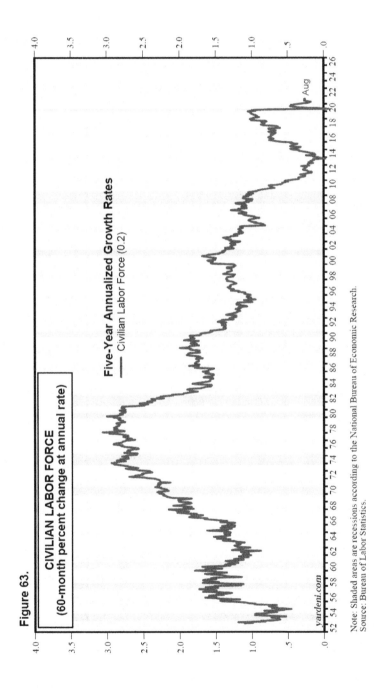

CIVILIAN LABOR FORCE
(60-month percent change at annual rate)

Five-Year Annualized Growth Rates
—— Civilian Labor Force (0.2)

yardeni.com

Note: Shaded areas are recessions according to the National Bureau of Economic Research.
Source: Bureau of Labor Statistics.

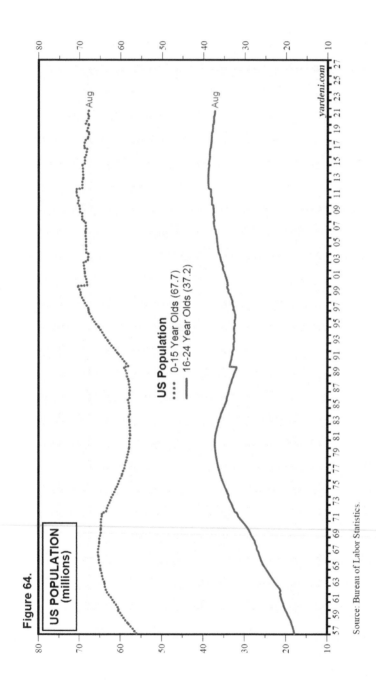

Figure 64.

US POPULATION
(millions)

US Population
••• 0-15 Year Olds (67.7)
—— 16-24 Year Olds (37.2)

Aug

Aug

Source: Bureau of Labor Statistics.

yardeni.com

Figure 65.

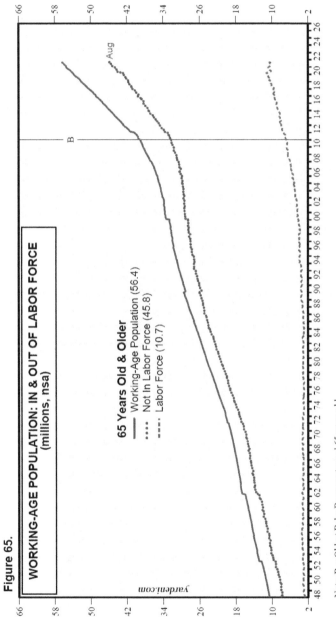

WORKING-AGE POPULATION: IN & OUT OF LABOR FORCE
(millions, nsa)

65 Years Old & Older
— Working-Age Population (56.4)
••• Not In Labor Force (45.8)
■ ■ ■ Labor Force (10.7)

B

Aug

yardeni.com

Note: B = Oldest Baby Boomers turned 65 years old.
Source: Bureau of Labor Statistics.

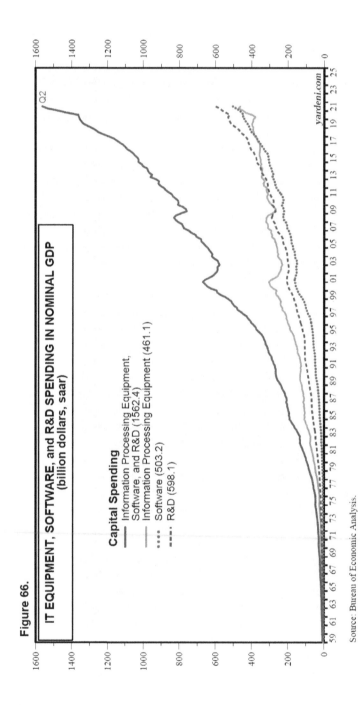

Figure 66.

IT EQUIPMENT, SOFTWARE, and R&D SPENDING IN NOMINAL GDP
(billion dollars, saar)

Capital Spending
—— Information Processing Equipment,
    Software, and R&D (1562.4)
—— Software (503.2)
—— Information Processing Equipment (461.1)
⋯⋯ R&D (598.1)

Source: Bureau of Economic Analysis.

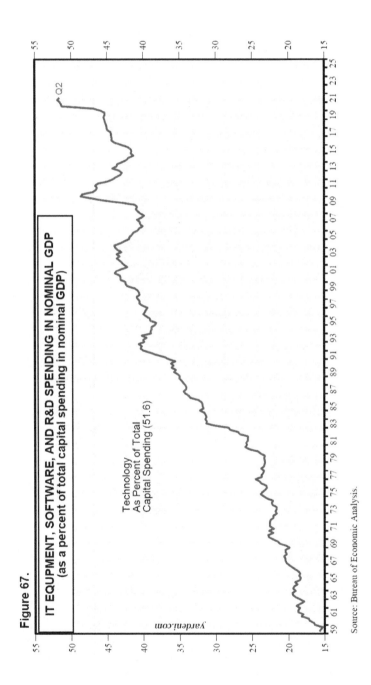

Figure 67.

IT EQUPMENT, SOFTWARE, AND R&D SPENDING IN NOMINAL GDP
(as a percent of total capital spending in nominal GDP)

Technology
As Percent of Total
Capital Spending (51.6)

Q2

Source: Bureau of Economic Analysis.

yardeni.com

Figure 68.

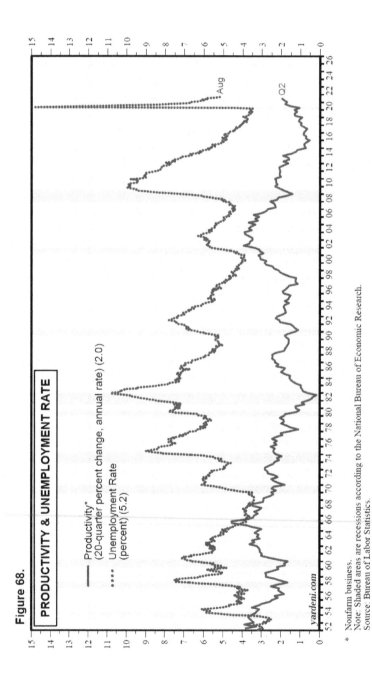

PRODUCTIVITY & UNEMPLOYMENT RATE

Productivity*
(20-quarter percent change, annual rate) (2.0)

Unemployment Rate
(percent) (5.2)

yardeni.com

* Nonfarm business.
Note: Shaded areas are recessions according to the National Bureau of Economic Research.
Source: Bureau of Labor Statistics.

Figure 69.

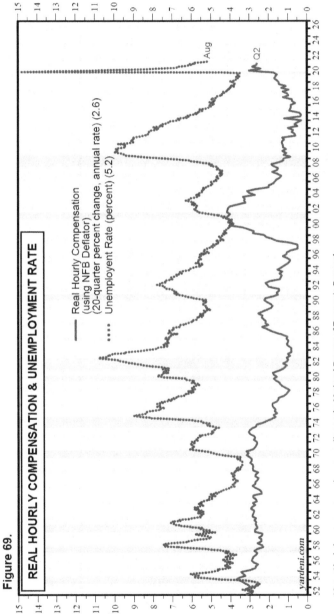

REAL HOURLY COMPENSATION & UNEMPLOYMENT RATE

— Real Hourly Compensation
   (using NFB Deflator)
   (20-quarter percent change, annual rate) (2.6)
···· Unemployent Rate (percent) (5.2)

vardeni.com

Note: Shaded areas are recessions according to the National Bureau of Economic Research.
Source: Bureau of Labor Statistics.

Figure 70.

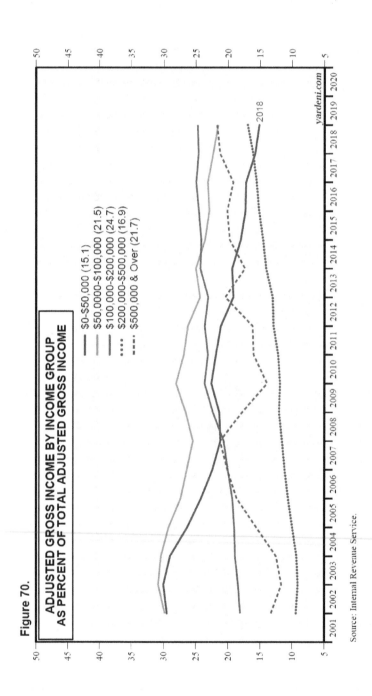

ADJUSTED GROSS INCOME BY INCOME GROUP
AS PERCENT OF TOTAL ADJUSTED GROSS INCOME

$0-$50,000 (15.1)
$50,0000-$100,000 (21.5)
$100,000-$200,000 (24.7)
$200,000-$500,000 (16.9)
$500,000 & Over (21.7)

Source: Internal Revenue Service.

Figure 71.

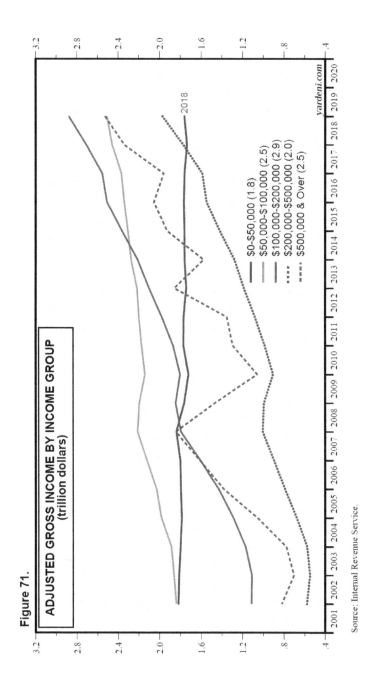

ADJUSTED GROSS INCOME BY INCOME GROUP
(trillion dollars)

Source: Internal Revenue Service.

Figure 72.

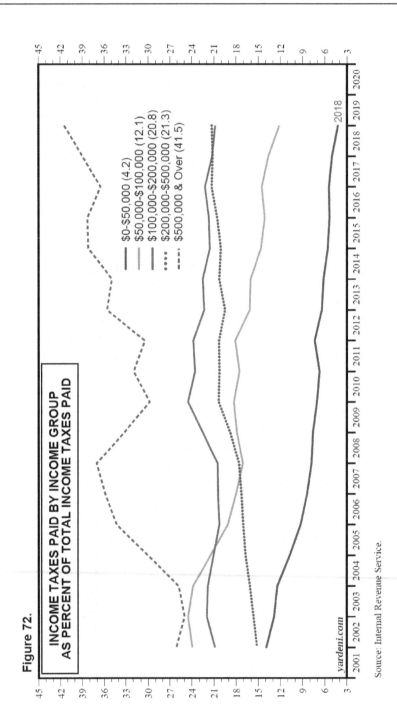

INCOME TAXES PAID BY INCOME GROUP
AS PERCENT OF TOTAL INCOME TAXES PAID

$0-$50,000 (4.2)
$50,000-$100,000 (12.1)
$100,000-$200,000 (20.8)
$200,000-$500,000 (21.3)
$500,000 & Over (41.5)

yardeni.com

Source: Internal Revenue Service.

Figure 73.

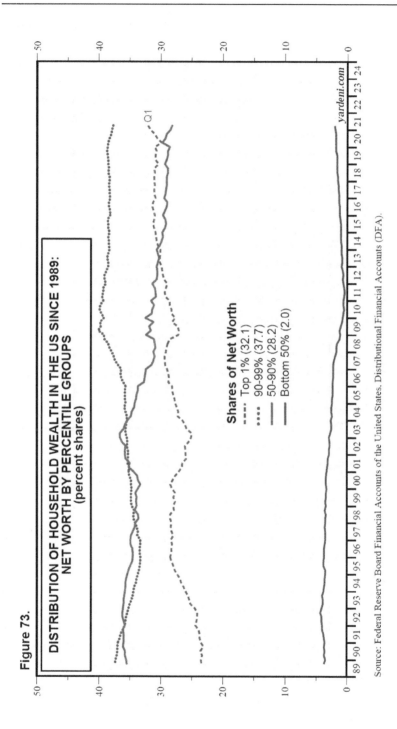

DISTRIBUTION OF HOUSEHOLD WEALTH IN THE US SINCE 1989:
NET WORTH BY PERCENTILE GROUPS
(percent shares)

Shares of Net Worth
- - - Top 1% (32.1)
· · · · 90-99% (37.7)
—— 50-90% (28.2)
—— Bottom 50% (2.0)

Source: Federal Reserve Board Financial Accounts of the United States. Distributional Financial Accounts (DFA).

Figure 74.

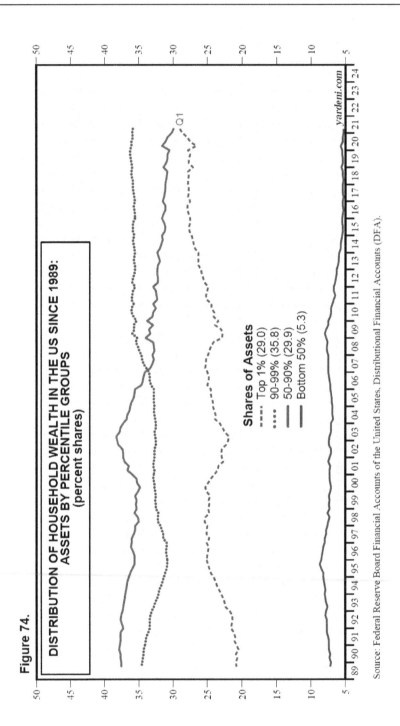

DISTRIBUTION OF HOUSEHOLD WEALTH IN THE US SINCE 1989:
ASSETS BY PERCENTILE GROUPS
(percent shares)

Shares of Assets
Top 1% (29.0)
90-99% (35.8)
50-90% (29.9)
Bottom 50% (5.3)

Source: Federal Reserve Board Financial Accounts of the United States, Distributional Financial Accounts (DFA).

Figure 75.

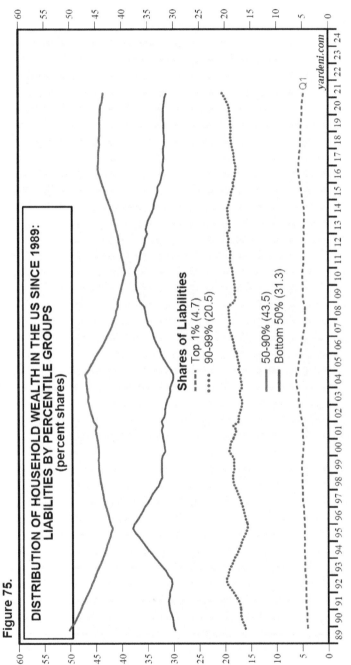

DISTRIBUTION OF HOUSEHOLD WEALTH IN THE US SINCE 1989:
LIABILITIES BY PERCENTILE GROUPS
(percent shares)

Shares of Liabilities
- - - Top 1% (4.7)
• • • • 90-99% (20.5)

—— 50-90% (43.5)
—— Bottom 50% (31.3)

yardeni.com

Source: Federal Reserve Board Financial Accounts of the United States. Distributional Financial Accounts (DFA).

Figure 76.

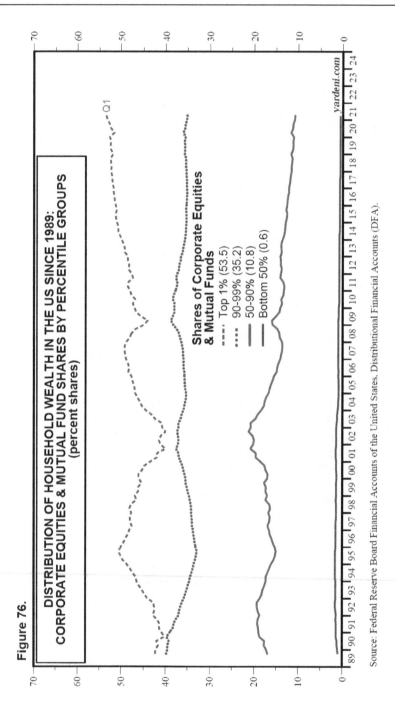

DISTRIBUTION OF HOUSEHOLD WEALTH IN THE US SINCE 1989:
CORPORATE EQUITIES & MUTUAL FUND SHARES BY PERCENTILE GROUPS
(percent shares)

Shares of Corporate Equities
& Mutual Funds
-■-■- Top 1% (53.5)
••••••• 90-99% (35.2)
——— 50-90% (10.8)
——— Bottom 50% (0.6)

Q1

yardeni.com

Source: Federal Reserve Board Financial Accounts of the United States. Distributional Financial Accounts (DFA).

Figure 77.

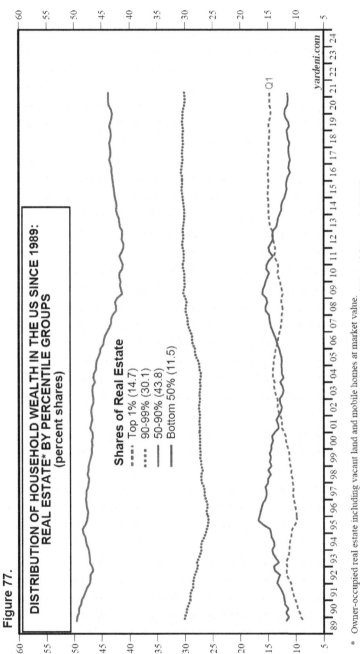

DISTRIBUTION OF HOUSEHOLD WEALTH IN THE US SINCE 1989:
REAL ESTATE* BY PERCENTILE GROUPS
(percent shares)

Shares of Real Estate
- - - Top 1% (14.7)
· · · · 90-99% (30.1)
──── 50-90% (43.8)
──── Bottom 50% (11.5)

* Owner-occupied real estate including vacant land and mobile homes at market value.
Source: Federal Reserve Board Financial Accounts of the United States. Distributional Financial Accounts (DFA).

Figure 78.

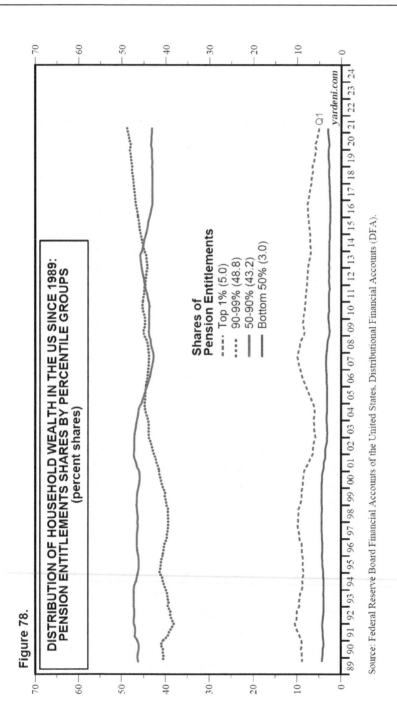

DISTRIBUTION OF HOUSEHOLD WEALTH IN THE US SINCE 1989: PENSION ENTITLEMENTS SHARES BY PERCENTILE GROUPS
(percent shares)

**Shares of
Pension Entitlements**
- - - Top 1% (5.0)
······ 90-99% (48.8)
—— 50-90% (43.2)
—— Bottom 50% (3.0)

yardeni.com

Source: Federal Reserve Board Financial Accounts of the United States. Distributional Financial Accounts (DFA).

Figure 79.

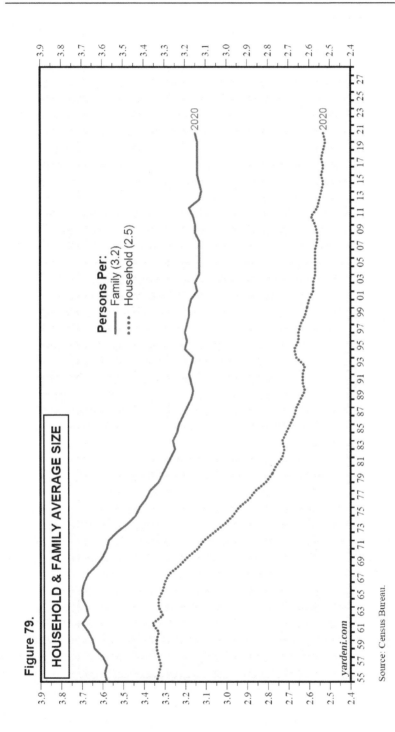

HOUSEHOLD & FAMILY AVERAGE SIZE

Persons Per:
— Family (3.2)
···· Household (2.5)

Source: Census Bureau.

yardeni.com

Figure 80.

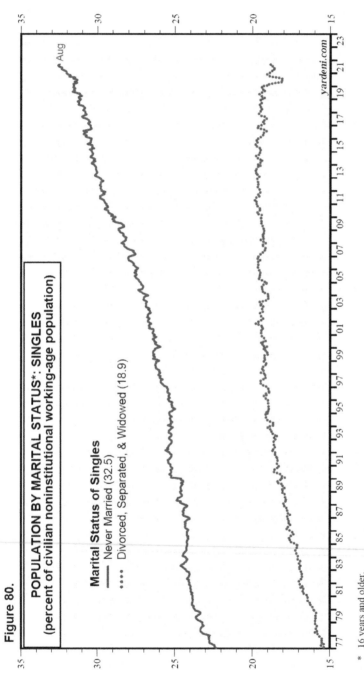

POPULATION BY MARITAL STATUS*: SINGLES
(percent of civilian noninstitutional working-age population)

Marital Status of Singles
—— Never Married (32.5)
••••• Divorced, Separated, & Widowed (18.9)

Figure 81.

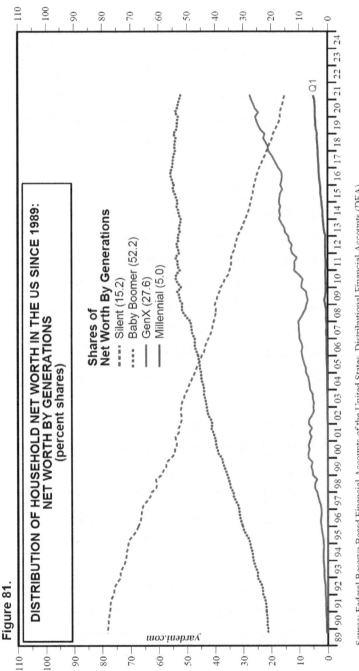

DISTRIBUTION OF HOUSEHOLD NET WORTH IN THE US SINCE 1989: NET WORTH BY GENERATIONS
(percent shares)

Shares of Net Worth By Generations
- Silent (15.2)
- Baby Boomer (52.2)
- GenX (27.6)
- Millennial (5.0)

Source: Federal Reserve Board Financial Accounts of the United States, Distributional Financial Accounts (DFA).

Figure 82.

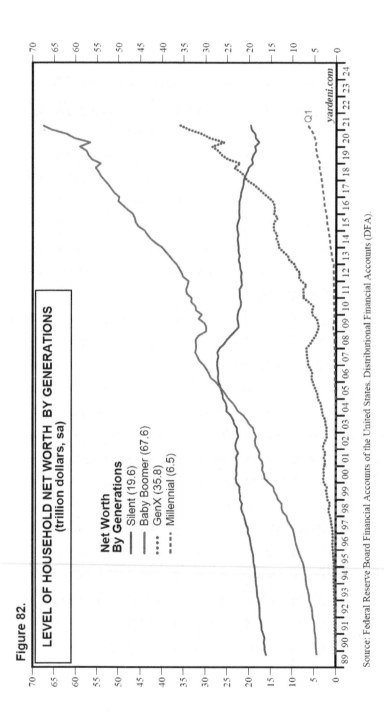

LEVEL OF HOUSEHOLD NET WORTH BY GENERATIONS
(trillion dollars, sa)

**Net Worth
By Generations**
— Silent (19.6)
— Baby Boomer (67.6)
•••• GenX (35.8)
– – – Millennial (6.5)

Source: Federal Reserve Board Financial Accounts of the United States, Distributional Financial Accounts (DFA).

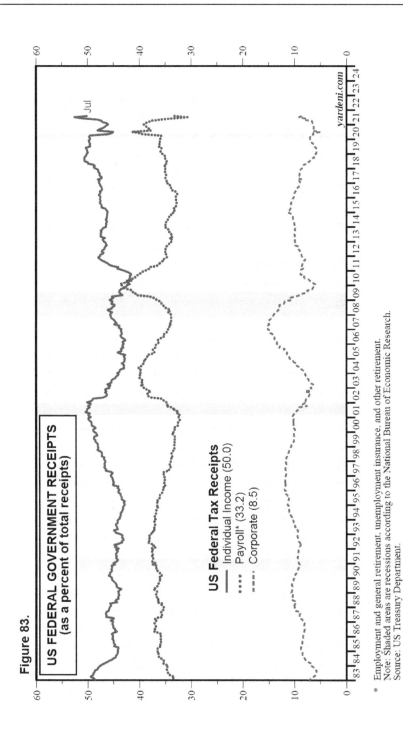

Figure 83.

US FEDERAL GOVERNMENT RECEIPTS
(as a percent of total receipts)

US Federal Tax Receipts
—— Individual Income (50.0)
•••• Payroll* (33.2)
---- Corporate (8.5)

Jul

yardeni.com

* Employment and general retirement. unemployment insurance. and other retirement.
Note: Shaded areas are recessions according to the National Bureau of Economic Research.
Source: US Treasury Department.

Figure 84.

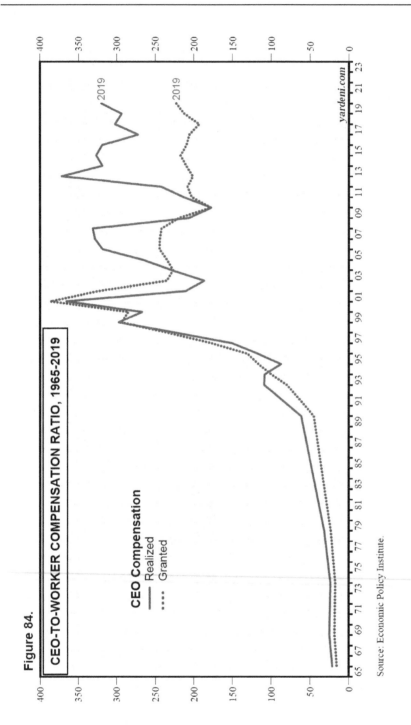

CEO-TO-WORKER COMPENSATION RATIO, 1965-2019

CEO Compensation
—— Realized
···· Granted

Source: Economic Policy Institute.

yardeni.com

Figure 85.

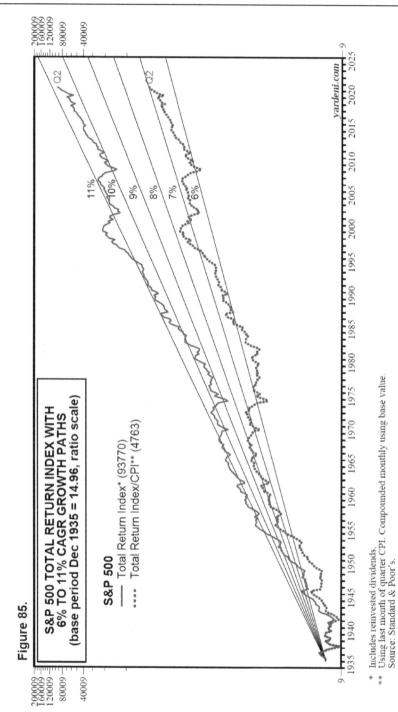

S&P 500 TOTAL RETURN INDEX WITH
6% TO 11% CAGR GROWTH PATHS
(base period Dec 1935 = 14.96, ratio scale)

S&P 500
—— Total Return Index* (93770)
···· Total Return Index/CPI** (4763)

* Includes reinvested dividends.
** Using last month of quarter CPI. Compounded monthly using base value.
Source: Standard & Poor's.

yardeni.com

Notes

Linked endnotes can be found at
www.yardenibook.com/studies.

Introduction

1. Burton W. Folsom, *The Myth of the Robber Barons: A New Look at the Rise of Big Business in America*, Young America's Foundation (2018).

Chapter 1: The Prosperity Economy

2. Adam Smith, *An Inquiry into the Nature & Causes of the Wealth of Nations*, Chapter II, "Of the Principle which Gives Occasion to the Division of Labour," 1776, Gutenberg.org.
3. Adam Smith, *An Inquiry into the Nature & Causes of the Wealth of Nations*, Chapter X, "Of Wages and Profit in the Different Employments of Labour and Stock," 1776, Gutenberg.org.

Chapter 2: The Profits Cycle

4. Irving Fisher, "The Debt-Deflation Theory of Great Depressions," *Econometrica*, 1933.
5. Ben Bernanke, Mark Gertler, and Simon Gilchrist, "The Financial Accelerator and the Flight to Quality," Working Paper No. 4789, National Bureau of Economic Research, July 1994.
6. Ben S. Bernanke, "The Financial Accelerator and the Credit Channel," speech at The Credit Channel of Monetary Policy in the Twenty-first Century Conference, Federal Reserve Bank of Atlanta, Atlanta, Georgia, June 15, 2007.
7. Joe Abbott and I explain forward earnings in our *S&P 500 Earnings, Valuation, and the Pandemic* (2020) study.

Chapter 3: What's Wrong with This Picture?

8. Find it on my Amazon Author Page.
9. Edward Yardeni and Joseph Abbott, Appendix 2: "S&P 500 Price Index, Revenues & Earnings Data Series," *S&P 500 Earnings, Valuation, and the Pandemic* (2020).

10. Bureau of Economic Analysis, Chapter 13: "Corporate Profits" in *NIPA Handbook: Concepts and Methods of the U.S. National Income and Product Accounts*, December 2020.

11. Edward Yardeni and Joseph Abbott, *Stock Buybacks: The True Story* (2019).

Chapter 4: Ins and Outs of Profits

12. Internal Revenue Service, "Forming a Corporation" webpage.

13. Internal Revenue Service, "Some S corporations may want to convert to C corporations" webpage.

14. Bureau of Economic Analysis, Chapter 13: "Corporate Profits" in *NIPA Handbook: Concepts and Methods of the U.S. National Income and Product Accounts*, December 2020.

15. Internal Revenue Service, "S Corporations" webpage.

16. Brookings, "9 facts about pass-through businesses," May 15, 2017.

17. Bureau of Economic Analysis, "Why is the estimate of NIPA dividends as a share of corporate profits much larger than the share reported in private-sector estimates?" webpage.

18. Bureau of Economic Analysis, "Where are the dividend measures shown in the national accounts?" webpage.

19. Internal Revenue Service, "Dividends (Distributions of Cash and Property) of S Corps and Other Corporations," Excel table.

20. Howard Krakower, Jennifer Lee, Kate Pinard, and Marlyn Rodriguez, "Prototype NIPA Estimates of Profits for S Corporations," Bureau of Economic Analysis, May 17, 2021.

21. Scott Eastman, "Corporate and Pass-Through Business Income and Returns Since 1980," Tax Foundation, April 23, 2019. See also Erica York, "Pass-Through Businesses Q&A," Tax Foundation, May 9, 2019.

22. Bureau of Economic Analysis, Chapter 11: "Nonfarm Proprietors' Income," in *NIPA Handbook: Concepts and Methods of the U.S. National Income and Product Accounts*, December 2020.

23. The household measure of employment counts the number of workers, while the payroll measure counts the number of jobs. Both are reported by the Bureau of Labor Statistics in its monthly Employment Report.

Chapter 5: Uses and Alleged Abuses of Profits

24. Chuck Schumer and Bernie Sanders, "Schumer and Sanders: Limit Corporate Stock Buybacks," *The New York Times*, February 3, 2019.

25. Edward Yardeni and Joseph Abbott, *Stock Buybacks: The True Story* (2019).

26. National Center for Employee Ownership, "Employee Ownership by the Numbers" website article, March 2021.

27. Carol E. Moylan, "Employee Stock Options and the National Economic Accounts," *BEA Briefing*, February 2008.

28. Andrew W. Hodge, "Comparing NIPA Profits With S&P 500 Profits," *BEA Briefing*, March 2011.

29. William Lazonick, "Profits Without Prosperity," *Harvard Business Review*, September 2014.

Chapter 6: Productivity and Prosperity

30. Lawrence H. Summers, "The Biden stimulus is admirably ambitious. But it brings some big risks, too," *The Washington Post*, February 4, 2021.
31. U.S. Chamber of Commerce, "U.S. Chamber Calls for Ending $300 Weekly Supplemental Unemployment Benefits to Address Labor Shortages," press release, May 7, 2021.
32. CNBC, Christina Wilkie, "Biden goes on offensive against economic critics, argues rising wages show his agenda is working," May 27, 2021.
33. Bureau of Labor Statistics, "Productivity and Costs" webpage.
34. For a comprehensive list along with definitions of this and alternative measures of wages and labor costs, see Ed Yardeni, "Alternative Measures of Wages & Labor Cost" in my 2018 book, *Predicting the Markets: A Professional Autobiography*.
35. Economic Policy Institute (EPI) webpage. The EPI is heavily supported by unions. Until he passed away in August 2021, the chairman of its board of directors was Richard L. Trumka, the president of the AFL-CIO. The following unions are also represented on the EPI's board of directors: USW, UAW, SEIU, IAM, AFSCME, CWA, and AFT. The self-described "nonpartisan" group also counts the chair of the Democratic National Committee on its board.
36. Economic Policy Institute, "About" webpage.
37. Economic Policy Institute, "The Productivity-Pay Gap" webpage, May 2021.
38. A footnote in the Federal Reserve's February 2000 *Monetary Policy Report* to Congress explained why the committee decided to switch to the inflation rate based on the PCE deflator rather than the CPI.
39. Drew DeSilver, "For most U.S. workers, real wages have barely budged in decades," Pew Research Center, August 7, 2018.
40. Joseph E. Stiglitz, "Progressive Capitalism Is Not an Oxymoron," *The New York Times*, April 19, 2019.
41. The Census Bureau uses the Consumer Price Index for all Urban Consumers Research Series (CPI-U-RS), provided by the Bureau of Labor Statistics for 1978 through 2019, to adjust for changes in the cost of living. For years prior to 1978, the Census Bureau used estimates provided by the Bureau of Labor Statistics from the CPI-U-X1 series. The CPI-U-X1 is an experimental series that preceded the CPI-U-RS and estimated the inflation rate in the Consumer Price Index for all Urban Consumers (CPI-U). See Appendix A: "Estimates of Income," *Income and Poverty in the United States: 2019*, United States Census Bureau, September 2020.
42. For more on the Great Inflation, see the excerpt of Chapter 3 of my 2018 book, *Predicting the Markets: A Professional Autobiography*.

43. Bank of America, "Bank of America Increases US Minimum Hourly Wage to $25 by 2025" press release, May 18, 2021.

44. Jack E. Triplett, "The Solow Productivity Paradox: What Do Computers Do to Productivity?" Brookings Institution, May 20, 1998.

45. George Westinghouse won the bid to light the 1893 World's Fair: Columbian Exposition in Chicago with alternating current. In a building devoted to electrical exhibits, he demonstrated to the American public the safety, reliability, and efficiency of a fully integrated alternating current system. See Wikipedia.

Chapter 7: Income and Wealth in America

46. Adjusted gross income (AGI) is defined by the Internal Revenue Service as total income (line 6, Form 1040) minus statutory adjustments (line 36, Schedule 1). Total income includes labor compensation, taxable interest, ordinary dividends, alimony, net capital gains, rents and royalties, distributive share of partnership or S corporation net income or loss, and several other smaller sources of income. Adjustments to income include such items as educator expenses, student loan interest, alimony payments, and contributions to a retirement account.

47. Jesse Eisinger, Jeff Ernsthausen, and Paul Kiel, "The Secret IRS Files: Trove of Never-Before-Seen Records Reveal How the Wealthiest Avoid Income Tax," ProPublica, June 8, 2021.

48. Batty, Michael, Jesse Bricker, Joseph Briggs, Elizabeth Holmquist, Susan McIntosh, Kevin Moore, Eric Nielsen, Sarah Reber, Molly Shatto, Kamila Sommer, Tom Sweeney, and Alice Henriques Volz, "Introducing the Distributional Financial Accounts of the United States," Finance and Economics Discussion Series 2019-017, Board of Governors of the Federal Reserve System, March 2019.

49. Lindsay Jacobs, Elizabeth Llanes, Kevin Moore, Jeffrey Thompson, and Alice Henriques Volz, "Wealth Concentration in the United States Using an Expanded Measure of Net Worth," Working Paper, August 2, 2021.

50. Emmanuel Saez and Gabriel Zucman, "The Rise of Income and Wealth Inequality in America: Evidence from Distributional Macroeconomic Accounts," NBER Working Paper No. 27922, October 2020.

Chapter 8: Profitable and Unprofitable Policies

51. Barack Obama, "Remarks by the President at a Campaign Event in Roanoke, Virginia," Office of the Press Secretary, The White House, July 13, 2012.

52. Daniel Indiviglio, "Why Businesses Should Fear Elizabeth Warren," *The Atlantic,* September 23, 2011.

53. Business Roundtable, "Business Roundtable Redefines the Purpose of a Corporation to Promote 'An Economy That Serves All Americans'," August 19, 2019.

54. The MBA Oath.

55. Council of Institutional Investors, "Council of Institutional Investors Responds to Business Roundtable Statement on Corporate Purpose," August 19, 2019.

56. Editorial Board, "The 'Stakeholder' CEOs," *The Wall Street Journal*, August 19, 2019.

57. Milton Friedman, "A Friedman doctrine—The Social Responsibility of Business Is to Increase Its Profits," *The New York Times*, September 13, 1970.

58. Allison Herren Lee, "Climate, ESG, and the Board of Directors: 'You Cannot Direct the Wind, But You Can Adjust Your Sails'," June 28, 2021 keynote speech at the 2021 Society for Corporate Governance National Conference.

59. Saijel Kishan, "How Wrong Was Milton Friedman? Harvard Team Quantifies the Ways," Bloomberg, December 1, 2020.

60. Saijel Kishan, "Corporate Climate Efforts Lack Impact, Say Former Sustainability Executives," Bloomberg Green, July 13, 2021.

61. Larry Fink, "A Fundamental Reshaping of Finance," 2020 letter addressed to CEOs.

62. Tariq Fancy, "Financial world greenwashing the public with deadly distraction in sustainable investing practices," *USA TODAY*, March 16, 2021.

63. Lisa Hagen, "McConnell: Businesses Using 'Economic Blackmail' to Alter Laws," *US News & World Report*, April 5, 2021.

64. Emily Cochrane, "Elizabeth Warren will propose a minimum tax on the nation's richest companies," *The New York Times*, August 9, 2021.

65. Lawrence Mishel and Jori Kandra, "CEO compensation surged 14% in 2019 to $21.3 million," Economic Policy Institute, August 18, 2020.

66. Dylan Matthews, "Bill Clinton tried to limit executive pay. Here's why it didn't work," *The Washington Post*, August 16, 2012.

67. Securities and Exchange Commission, "Investor Bulletin: Say-on-Pay and Golden Parachute Votes," March 2011.

68. Kristoffer Inton and Joshua Aguilar, "Board Members and CEOs: How Close Is Too Close?," Morningstar US Videos, July 8, 2021.

69. Robert J. Jackson, Jr., "Stock Buybacks and Corporate Cashouts," Securities and Exchange Commission, June 11, 2018 speech.

70. Jerome H. Powell, "New Economic Challenges and the Fed's Monetary Policy Review," August 27, 2020 at "Navigating the Decade Ahead: Implications for Monetary Policy," an economic policy symposium sponsored by the Federal Reserve Bank of Kansas City, Jackson Hole, Wyoming (via webcast).

71. Board of Governors of the Federal Reserve System, "2020 Statement on Longer-Run Goals and Monetary Policy Strategy," August 27, 2020.

72. CNBC, "S&P 500 doubles from its pandemic bottom, marking the fastest bull market rally since WWII," August 16, 2021.

Epilogue

73. YouTube, "Comrade Kaprugina delivers a scolding" clip from movie *Doctor Zhivago*.

Made in the USA
Las Vegas, NV
25 October 2021